Small Strawbale

Natural Homes,
Projects & Designs

Small Strawbale

Natural Homes, Projects & Designs

Bill Steen   Athena Swentzell Steen   Wayne J. Bingham

Gibbs Smith, Publisher
Salt Lake City

To Colleen. — Wayne

To my father, Ralph Swentzell, who inspired me to fearlessly build with strawbales at a time it was unheard of, and to do so with ingenuity, commonsense, and simplicity. — Athena

For Ralph, my friend and father-in-law, thanks. — Bill

First Edition
09 08 07 06 05   5 4 3 2 1

Text © 2005 Bill and Athena Steen and Wayne J. Bingham
Photographs © 2005 Bill and Athena Steen and as noted on page 202
Illustrations © 2005 Wayne J. Bingam

Published by
Gibbs Smith, Publisher
P.O. Box 667
Layton, Utah 84041

Orders: 1.800.748.5439
www.gibbs-smith.com

Cover design by Rudy Ramos
Interior design by Athena Steen
Printed and bound in Hong Kong

Library of Congress Cataloging-in-Publication Data

Steen, Bill.
Small strawbale : natural homes, projects & design / Bill and Athena Steen
and Wayne Bingham.—1st ed.
p. cm.
ISBN 1-58685-515-8
1. Straw bale houses. I. Steen, Athena Swentzell, 1961- . II. Bingham,
Wayne. III. Title.
TH4818.S77.S7434 2005
693'.997—dc22
2004022522

CONTENTS

INTRODUCTION

This book features a collection of small strawbale houses, tiny studios, meditation spaces, outbuildings, and landscape walls. Most of them are rather simple and rectangular in shape. For the most part, they wouldn't find their way into the average architectural coffee table book or magazine. They represent a different kind of beauty, one that is born of hard work, simplicity, and an attempt to reestablish a connection with nature. A result of simple dreams and modest pocketbooks, these strawbale structures have been built largely by the efforts of their owners. They are projects the average person can afford.

This collection of featured structures represents an attempt to build simply using good materials such as straw, earth, stone, and timber; conserve energy; and have fun in the process. These structures are reminders that building one's own home is a desire that for the most part is inherent in all creatures. It is only in recent times that we have begun to think of the process as something that we are incapable of doing and that needs to be delegated to experts and professionals. In no way are the structures contained herein presented as perfect examples of the best or ideal way to build. What they do represent are conscious and deliberate attempts by those hoping to rediscover the meaning of "shelter" and escape the unnecessary extravagance of modern, oversized houses and the soulless repetitiveness of mass-produced houses.

In addition to being a book about a specific building material, this guide is also very much about the way we build. Building a house can be one of the most traumatic events in people's lives. The process is often a struggle among the owners who want the biggest house they can get for the least amount of money and the builder and architect guided by their experience, practice, and interests. In the background is the bank, with its timeline of the construction loan, and the vigilant shadow of the building inspector. In the end, there is the inevitable gap between the estimate and what the project actually ends up costing. People often begin the process of building their dream home with the unrealistic expectation that, once it is built, their life will be drastically improved when in actuality many are forever scarred by the process.

In many ways, our modern lives have been disconnected from things that really matter and that have genuine value. Our buildings and houses reflect our preoccupation with size and our belief that more surface grandeur will satisfy our needs and wants. No longer a sensible shelter that has some degree of harmony with the natural world, the modern home has become quite something else as Wendell Berry describes in *The Unsettling of America: Culture and Agriculture* "with its array of gadgets and machines, all powered by energies that are destructive of land or air or water." He goes on to say that "connected to work, market, school, recreation, etc. by gasoline engines, the modern home is a veritable factory of waste and destruction. It is the mainstay of the economy of money. But within the economies of energy and nature, it is a catastrophe. It takes the world's goods and converts them into garbage, sewage and noxious fumes—for none of which we have found a use."

When it comes to energy consumption, it has been estimated that the building industry as a whole accounts for as much as 48 percent of all the U.S. energy produced and is responsible for as much as 46 percent of all U.S. carbon dioxide emissions annually. That is double any other major sector. This is incredibly significant when one realizes that houses and other buildings can be designed to use very small amounts of imported energy or none at all. The culture of the modern developed world, for the most part, builds as if there were little connection between a building, its surrounding environment, and the finite energy sources available. Clearly, larger houses and buildings usually consume more resources than smaller ones, both in construction and operation. However, a small house that hasn't been carefully thought out may use more energy than a larger one with a better design, better insulation, and better material choice. It is worth noting that since the 1950s houses have increased almost three times in size per family member.

This book serves as a reminder that there is a simpler and more equitable way to build, one that avoids unnecessarily large and complicated designs that attempt to make a statement about what is impressive, artistic, or natural while, at the same time, consuming a disproportionate share of the world's resources.

A home sized to meet genuine needs—built by the hands and inspired by the dreams of those who inhabit it—is much more likely to contain a richness of soul and spirit.

GARDEN WALLS & FENCES

*Adobe wall with carved stone arch.
Santa Fe, New Mexico.*

Garden or landscape walls define private outdoor space, create a visual screen, serve as a backdrop for flowers and trees, and can help make a setting more intimate. In addition, they can keep people and animals in or out of a defined space—such as deer or bears out of the garden or children off an adjacent vehicular thoroughfare. They can also act as a sound barrier to city noise.

A good place to begin is by investigating what materials are available in your area. Some appropriate choices are concrete block, rammed earth, adobe, recycled concrete chunks, stone, cob, and earth-filled bags. Some appropriate materials for fences include poles, bamboo, and reeds.

For many applications, living plants such as hedges, vines, bamboo, and cacti perform the task beautifully while possibly providing something edible or attracting a desirable variety of wildlife. Plants are low on the embodied energy scale and provide added benefits by absorbing carbon dioxide and giving off oxygen, providing evaporative cooling and channeling breezes in desired directions. While waiting for the vegetation to grow, un-plastered strawbales might be used as a temporary barrier. Clay and straw could be used to cap the wall. Be sure to fill all the cavities and joints with seed so that as the wall decomposes, it will give birth to more plants.

We've included a photo of a wall built out of concrete block. At first glance, block walls might not seem like a natural and green choice, but the amount of cement used to make the concrete block is about the same as that used to plaster most free-standing strawbale walls. In contrast to a plastered strawbale wall, concrete block walls often can be disassembled and reused.

An arched wall made by Kaki Hunter and Donald Kiffmeyer from sandbags filled with compacted earth. Moab, Utah.

MATTS & JUDY'S STRAWBALE WALL

Tucson, Arizona

Judy Knox and Matts Myhrman at a bale wall raising.

"We first built the walls to outline the rear of our property for several reasons. One was to provide a sense of security and privacy for Matts' elderly mother, Mildred, who lives next door. Her strawbale cottage opened near the alley that is used as a travel way for many vagrants, inebriated college students, loose animals, and service vehicles. We also wanted a protective backdrop against which to raise vegetables and flowers. And, as always, we wanted to experiment with wall-building techniques we had ruminated on for some time, as well as try out different mud and lime renders on its surfaces.

"The rear walls have succeeded in all ways. They have stood the test of eight years without a problem. The walls' foundation was comprised of two layers of gravel-filled grain (sand) bags imbedded into the ground. We stabilized the walls by tying carrizo (reed) stalks, placed on either side of the walls, together by sewing through the bales. We protected the top of the walls with a layer of foam insulation (to prevent condensation on the underside of the plastic), added a plastic drape, and then followed with a thick layer of cob topped by clay roofing tiles at an angle for drainage. The beautiful and functional walls curving along the rear border of our

homeplace have allowed us to turn our backyard into a private and lovely oasis in the midst of the city's chaos. Abundant with flowers, trees, vines, and edibles, as well as lizards, birds, and butterflies, our backyard is a sanctuary.

"When it came time to renovate the front yard five years later, we wanted to repeat the success we'd had with the backyard wall, but with a few changes. The clay roofing tiles we used on the backyard walls, in addition to being so aesthetically pleasing, had done a better-than-hoped-for job of protecting the top of the walls, so on our front walls we decided to eliminate the plastic and the foam insulation. We placed only thick layers of cob topped by the angled roofing tiles. Since these walls would be along the more public front side of our homeplace, we wanted to combine our need for security, privacy, and protected gardens with our desire to extend a feeling of welcome and pleasure to visitors and passersby. We purposefully landscaped between the wall and the street and decorated the street-side surfaces with Mexican tiles.

"We love living in the surround of these lovely and protective strawbale walls. Within the limited space of two small urban lots, they have enabled us to extend our outdoor living spaces to the property perimeters, creating areas for gatherings, quiet meditation, gardening, and everyday dining and visiting. They help quiet the noises and frenetic energies of the city, allowing us an abundant life within a small space."

—Judy Knox and Matts Myhrman

FREESTANDING STRAWBALE WALLS

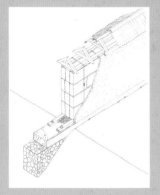

The primary concern with using strawbales for landscape walls is the often-limited longevity of the straw. If the plaster gets wet, the moisture can be drawn into the straw by capillary action or baked in by the sun. Moisture rising from the ground can also find its way into the straw. Once the moisture is in the straw core, the plaster shell is relatively impermeable to the passage of water vapor; it behaves like an inverted jar, preventing the moisture's ready escape. Over time, moisture can accumulate to levels that support microbial activity that can ultimately result in complete degradation of the straw core, leaving only a hollow plaster shell behind.

A cutaway of a freestanding strawbale wall.

USEFUL ELEMENTS TO INCORPORATE

• A foundation that keeps the bales and ideally the plaster above grade and allows for drainage.

• A roof or the equivalent to keep rain off the top of the wall and from running down the sides and to reduce sun exposure. Wood, metal, tiles, shingles, or thatch are all good material possibilities. The roof can also be thought of as an important aesthetic expression, but a specially designed roof will add to the complexity of construction as well as cost.

• A plaster that is at least vapor permeable enough to allow drying to take place should moisture find its way inside the wall. If the plaster is lime or cement, it would also be good to coat the plaster with something that prevents it from absorbing water but still allows water vapor to escape.

Earth-plastered strawbale wall protected with metal corrugated roofing. Patagonia, Arizona.

Lime-plastered strawbale wall with metal roof over entrance and a tile cap over the remaining wall. Patagonia, Arizona.

Un-plastered strawbales with a thatch roof of bear grass—nolina microcarpra, a traditional thatching material from southeastern Arizona and northern Mexico. Canelo, Arizona.

WAYNE & COLLEEN'S GARDEN WALL

The earth-plastered concrete block wall roofed with tiles encircles the backyard.

Salt Lake City, Utah

"Our garden wall started as a mere replacement for an old, failing, unreinforced concrete block retaining wall in our backyard. It was level with our ground, but it was holding 5 feet (1.52 meters) of earth from falling into the alley and our neighbor's yard. It was topped with a wire fence that kept pets from intruding, but it offered no visual or acoustical privacy. We could have just replaced the retaining wall and wire fence above, but we wanted to explore the effect of raising the wall an additional five feet. We hired an affable Polynesian group to build the wall. Wayne had just returned from a Canelo Project workshop and was enthusiastic about trying his newly acquired earthen plaster skills on the new block garden wall.

"Clay, sand, chopped straw, wheat paste, and linseed oil were mixed and applied to our side of the wall. The neighbor who shared the wall wanted 'real stucco' on her side until we had about a third of ours finished. 'Can you do that on my side of the wall too?' she asked. Yes, we did her wall. We also helped to construct an additional set of walls to fully enclose her yard.

"What started as a retaining wall replacement became a personal expression as the enclosure gave our backyard a new, unique feeling. The

A wrought-iron gate incorporated into the wall.

color of straw tied the wall back to the land. We reduced the size of our lawn and increased the size of the flower and vegetable garden, which are profiled against the wall. We installed recycled, glazed tile caps on top of the wall to keep the rain and snow from eroding the plaster. We used metal grilles to separate portions of the wall because we wanted to enjoy each other's yard.

"The walls and the garden have been grown in beauty. They have given us great satisfaction and a deep sense of place. We now have a refuge from the city. The plaster has fared well over the past five years. However, extending it all the way to the ground was a mistake because rain and snow were absorbed by the plaster. We corrected this by cutting it back eight inches. An overzealous lawn sprinkler system has also created some mold spots that we corrected with hydrogen peroxide spray."

—Wayne J. Bingham and Colleen Smith
www.wjbingham.com

THIN SHELL CEMENT & WIRE WALLS

Wall built using a rebar frame, covered with metal lath, and coated with cement-based stucco. Ferro cement could also be used.

One idea that has surfaced over the years in discussions among strawbale enthusiasts is the feasibility of building a faux or somewhat streamlined strawbale wall. Conceivably one might create the shape of a strawbale wall using a frame of rebar, cover it with metal lath or building paper-backed wire, and plaster it. In other words, no bales, no foundation, but instead a cement shell like those Ferro cement dinosaurs or teepees one used to see driving along Route 66 in days gone by. Building such a wall in a sinusoidal or zigzag pattern would add to its stability. We are purposefully avoiding any specific guidelines about how to build such a wall but offer the idea here as food for the imagination. So as not to limit this type of application to that of creating an inverse shell that looks like a strawbale wall, the same approach can be used to create a single wythe wall.

Core of thin cement wall with a rebar frame and expanded metal lath.

Thin curving cement and metal lath wall at the cohousing project "Stone Curves." Colored with ferrous sulfate. Tucson, Arizona.

FENCES & SCREENS

A woven fence of carrizo (Arrondo donax). *Sonora, Mexico.*

Around the world, one finds an amazing variety of fences made from local plant materials. These range from very formal and intricate ones, like the bamboo fences of Japan, to much more rustic examples, like the ocotillo cactus fence found in the southwestern United States and Mexico.

A full-blown, free-standing wall built largely from masonry materials isn't always necessary, especially when there is no need for a sound barrier from traffic or a retaining wall. A fence is useful as a visual screen or partition. Not needing foundations or plastering, fences are typically much less expensive than walls.

Consider any number of locally available materials that serve quite nicely in these types of situations. Instead of going down to the building supply store to buy something that has been industrially processed and transported, and that needs to be assembled with additional manufactured materials. These include poles, branches, bamboos, and reeds. With a little ingenuity and imagination, there is an infinite variety of patterns and textures that can be created.

It is also possible to literally grow a fence or screen. There are many plants that can be propagated from cuttings or plants that can be put directly into the ground to take root, grow, and even bloom.

Top, left: A juniper-pole fence. Santa Clara, New Mexico.

Bottom, left: A divider made from dried saguaro cactus trunks. Home of Matts Myhrman and Judy Knox. Tucson, Arizona.

Top, middle: Fence of carrizo (arrondo donax) with vines growing through it at the home of Matts Myhrman and Judy Knox. Tucson, Arizona.

Bottom, left: A living fence of cottonwood trees with smaller branches woven through the trunks. Sonora, Mexico.

Top, right: A juniper-pole fence defines the entrance. Canelo, Arizona.

Bottom, right: A screen of woven reed mats. Tucson, Arizona.

15

TOM & SATOMI'S BAMBOO ENTRY GATE & FENCE

Kingston, New Mexico

"Bamboo is an inspiration to many as a living plant and, in our case, a building material. In the Asian worlds, bamboo has many uses; in this country, it has yet to achieve its potential. For us, pinning strawbale walls with bamboo has grown quite popular. In Asia, the beauty of bamboo can be seen in garden fences and gates.

"Traveling through Japan with Satomi and her family and seeing these fences firsthand was all I needed for inspiration. I combined that with inspiration from a number of Japanese garden books; my favorite is *Building Bamboo Fences* by Isao Yoshida. In the preface, Isao states that his book is an introduction to bamboo fence-building techniques. Maybe so, but for me the color photos, detailed drawings, sketches, and the fact that it is in English make it one of my most cherished books on bamboo in my library.

"Curb appeal, aesthetics, and details mean a lot to me. For Satomi, a fence represents hidden treasures beyond. I decided to build a bamboo gate, fence, and entry gate. The project was a good opportunity to use up my collection of rusted steel and try out my amateur welding skills. We used 360 5/8-inch-diameter (15.88-millimeter-diameter) poles all attached with leftover heavy gauge copper electrical wire. Satomi installed the poles, and I went back through and did the twisting. Later she painted on a coating of linseed oil, and I capped off the tops with copper water pipe sliced in half. (That was fun!) The final touch was adding the split horizontal rails, which Satomi tied on with the traditional and authentic dyed twine we brought back from Japan.

"For us, there is a special feeling we get everytime we open the gate and see the hidden beauty."

—Tom Lander
www.landerland.com

Tom and Satomi in front of their bamboo gate.

Opposite: A red plastered fence abuts the bamboo entry gate. There's a bamboo planted in front, which can be harvested in the future.

OPEN-AIR STRUCTURES

A window opening molded with straw–clay plaster. Canelo, Arizona.

Open-air structures partially enclose spaces or shelter spaces that accommodate a wide variety of functions such as seating, working, and storage. They are great starter projects since they are typically small as well as non-threatening in terms of complexity and cost. They are somewhat akin to a primeval shelter and therefore intuitive. Just about anyone can build one without fear of major structural failure.

Since these structures are not intended to be enclosed, airtight, and highly insulated, they provide great opportunities to experiment with creative materials and techniques. They can be a place to play and have fun. There is a freedom from seriousness that accompanies the building of one's "real house." Undertakings that on larger or more expensive structures would be too time-consuming or overwhelming—such as collecting stones from the nearby wash for a dry stacked foundation, cutting poles or bamboo for the roof, or harvesting reeds and grasses for thatch—suddenly become feasible. Playful open-air structures can serve as wonderful teaching tools to learn about a wide range of natural materials, including strawbales, clay blocks, cob, paints, and plasters.

Whether in the backyard, the back forty, or in the garden, people are instinctively drawn to these outdoor structures. As natural focal points, a whole array of activities, such as cooking, eating, and sleeping, seem to radiate around them. They may even inspire your family, a neighborhood kid, or the curious to join in and help you build the structure.

An earth-plastered cob sitting area with inlaid tiles in northern California is protected from rain with a flaring bamboo roof structure. The gutter off the front edge is also made of bamboo. Built by DeBoer Architects (www.deboerarchitects.com).

THE BUS STOP

Canelo, Arizona

The seat is made from small hand-made loaves of cob filled in behind with compacted dirt capped with plaster.

"We live so far off the beaten track that the bus will most likely never make a stop at this little structure. Nevertheless, the Bus Stop was so-nicknamed for its appearance. This covered structure is used extensively for seating during our workshops and as a practice palette for participants to try out different paints and plasters. Over the years, it's been covered with multiple coats of different types of clay and casein paints. Whenever a new mix needs to be tested, it's the Bus Stop that is usually the recipient. Consequently, it gets a new look on a regular basis—some are better than others.

"The Bus Stop was originally built during a workshop. Just about all the materials used in its construction are local. We used wheat strawbales from a local farmer to create the structure, nearby clay soils for the plaster, stones for the foundation, and juniper poles from our property for the posts and roof structure. The metal roofing and 1 x 4-inch (25.40 x 101.60-millimeter) purlins are the only materials that weren't locally made."

—Bill and Athena Steen

The lizard, duck, and arched niche were sculpted from clay and straw, and then painted with clay and wheat paste.

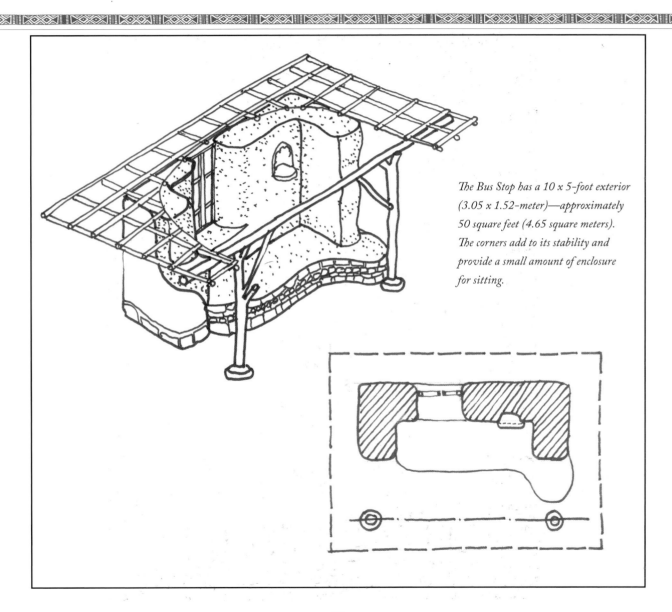

The Bus Stop has a 10 x 5-foot exterior (3.05 x 1.52-meter)—approximately 50 square feet (4.65 square meters). The corners add to its stability and provide a small amount of enclosure for sitting.

PLASTERING WITH EARTH

When it comes to plasters, clay is one of the most gorgeous and fascinating of all building materials. It is simultaneously complex and simple. Its finish can be smoothed, textured, polished, or left rough and sculpted artistically into beautiful shapes and patterns. Children can have fun with it, and the most skilled of craftsmen can use it to create some of the finest work imaginable. African women use clay to sculpt and plaster exquisitely finished walls using only their hands and stones, while Japanese plaster craftsmen utilize a large variety of complex plastering tools, some made of steel reminiscent of the material used to make the finest Japanese Samurai swords.

From a practical and functional standpoint, there are characteristics of clay that are somewhat challenging and others that make it highly desirable. Not only are there many types of clay, different types of clay behave very differently. Some have more binding ability, while others are more expansive, meaning that they shrink more when drying and are more prone to cracking. However, good plasters can be developed with the addition of sufficient aggregate and/or fiber in combination with time, patience, and experimentation.

Clay can be found almost anywhere in the world and often costs nothing or next to nothing. Since clay is a non-manufactured material, it is about as nontoxic and natural as you can get. Additionally, it effectively absorbs both pollutants and excess humidity, and is considered alive by many.

Since all earthen materials are not water-resistant unless fired, clay plasters should be protected from exposure to rain. Clay can be successfully used on the interior of a building and outside under the cover of a porch. In moderate climates, with the addition of a stabilizing material, clay can make a serviceable exterior plaster. It will take trial and experimentation to discover what will be successful.

Workshop participants mixing plaster by hand; Steen children Arjuna, Benito, and Kalin, and their mother, Athena, mixing and plastering; Ruth Lopez from Obregon, Mexico; and plaster-craftsman Syuhei Hasado from Japan.

25

JOELEE'S CANTINA

Tucson, Arizona

"This little structure was envisioned as a much needed social space on the DAWN SouthWest site—my home. This vision was translated into reality over two years in separate workshops conducted by Athena and Bill Steen. As always, seeing how the Steens live their lives and how they work in a very real way inspired us to get into this work, not just with our hands, but also with our hearts.

"On a cool weekend in November 2001, some twenty-five workshop participants put up this low-cost, but very useful, cantina from the footer to the roof. A year later, a workshop group learning paints and finishes completed and transformed it, demonstrating the amazing colors that can come from natural materials. Children participated in the painting, leaving behind handprints that sparkle with mica—little invitations to touch and feel the materials.

"The cantina has survived a major storm and winds that ripped up trailers and roofs in the area in the summer of 2003. Since the structure is made of plaster with heavy straw, the blasting wind and rain could not penetrate deeply, though a 'hairy' strawbale look now prevails on some edges. Clay-lime plaster is being applied in stages to prevent further weathering.

"Rain or shine, people are drawn to *La Cantina de Paja,* and it is filled with laughter and good spirits time and again as they enjoy coffee and good company. It has been chosen as the site of birthday parties, honored with Italian arias and fine art, and blessed with the great meals baked in the adjoining bread oven with all the ambiance of old Mexico."

—Joelee Joyce
DAWN SouthWest/Out on Bale by Mail
www.caneloproject.com/dawn/

Top, left: Blue ice tea bottles molded into a window decorated with clay.

Top, right: Joelee Joyce with her dog, Dulce.

Opposite, bottom left: Joelee runs and hosts several workshops throughout the year.

KIM'S SUMMER KITCHEN

Ship Harbour, Nova Scotia

Kim finishes plastering
her clay oven.

Opposite: Built in
1995, the kitchen is
20 x 8 feet (6.10 x
2.44 meters) with a
gravel-bag foundation.
It has three to four
courses of bales, a liv-
ing roof, and earthen
plasters with myriad
finishes.

"small now.
Small is, so often, central.

It is the touchstone we finger in our pocket that
grounds us and guides us.

The kernel, the nucleus, the heart of matters
counts.

"Small are the shelters and shapes in the family
compound that reflect who we are and where
we have been.

Small is the wing in these woods that holds
our community hearth.

Small feet, small hands, squishing; tiny
tongues tasting.

Summer kitchen, gathering place. Pizza,
laughter, inspiration place.

"Dragon morphed fish with mirrored scales, the
nature of clay.

Gift of our friendship. Container of learning.
Thin edge of the wedge, never looking back.

"Workshop memories,
I think none of us realized in those northern
lake days, and loon cry nights where all this was
headed.

Or perhaps we did.

Start small, trust, and play. Ask questions.
Do it. Add a detail.
      beautiful. small. now."

—Kim Thompson
shipharbour@ns.sympatico.ca
www.naturalbuilding.ca
www.chebucto.ns.ca/Culture/
   Shifting_Boundaries

EARTHEN BAKING OVENS

It's hard to imagine that for so little expenditure of money and labor a clay oven can give back so much enjoyment and benefit. A simple oven costs next to nothing to make, especially if you're using local materials, such as stone for the base and clay for the body of the oven. The only expense might be the price of firebrick for baking directly on the hearth.

Traditionally, most clay or masonry ovens are used for bread, but pizza from a wood-fired oven is extraordinary and a turkey comes out full of flavor in half the time. This type of oven bakes by retained heat: wood is first burned in the chamber of the oven, the ashes are then removed, and finally the food is left to bake. This type of oven bakes using the heat retained by the thermal mass of the earthen materials comprising the oven itself. One exception is pizza that also uses direct heat from the fire that continues to burn in the oven while it is baked. Ovens made of earthen or masonry materials can be built in many different ways, but some materials can have weaknesses that will make them less efficient.

The oven shown here is based on clay ovens from Quebec, Canada, that were built using a vernacular French design hundreds of years old. The oven has an oval floor plan, a low roof/door, and a no smoke-hole vent. Air enters through the open door and exits through the door as the oven burns. Authors Lise Boily and Jean-Francois Blanchette first

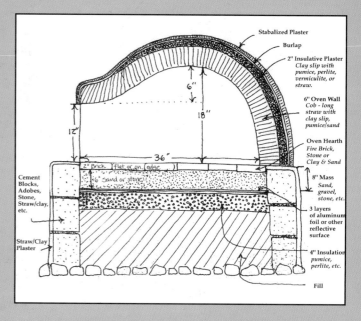

published the design criteria in their book *The Bread Ovens of Quebec.* Oven-builder Alan Scott, in the book *The Bread Builders,* coauthored with Daniel Wing, concisely distilled the same information. Although their book focuses on much more complicated and expensive brick ovens, the design principles are the same. This book also contains information about clay ovens. Kiko Denzer's book *Build Your Own Earth Oven* contains helpful information about building and sculpting ovens with clay.

These earthen baking ovens are slightly longer than they are wide with the door making up approximately 63 percent

of the oven dome. The base can be built from a variety of materials, including concrete block, stone, wood, and adobe. A waist-high hearth makes baking easier. The hearth and floor of the oven need slightly more mass than the walls. An oven for occasional use might have 6 inches (152.40 millimeters) in the dome and a total of 7 inches (177.80 millimeters) in the hearth. The hearth can be built using firebrick over stone, gravel, or concrete if baking directly on it; otherwise, a clay floor is adequate.

The Quebec ovens were built using a mixture of clay soil and straw over a formwork of branches, but a sand mold also works well. The oven, both hearth and dome, need to be wrapped with an insulating material, such as pumice or vermiculite, and covered with burlap before plastering. The exterior of the oven can be sculpted to one's desire. Because these ovens are made of clay, rain and frost will cause the surface to erode. In Quebec, roofs and small shelters covered the ovens.

Top, left: Juanita Morales cleaning the coals out of her hot oven.
Top, right: Quebec earthen oven with iron cast doors under an A-frame roof.

JUANITA'S LAUNDRY ROOM

Obregon, Sonora, Mexico

The interior is painted with clay paints. The floor is made of cement pavers set into loose gravel to ensure good drainage. It has a built-in bamboo drying rack and shelves.

"One winter we were working on the Save the Children office building in Obregon, Sonora, Mexico, along with a group of workshop participants. We needed a project for the group that could be finished in a little more than a week. Our friend and host Juanita Morales desperately needed a protected area, out of the sun and wind, where she could do her laundry in comfort. Since many Mexican families still use a concrete basin or scrub board, this little building had to be large enough to house the basin, a washing machine, and a table for folding the clothes. Building this structure made a wonderful workshop project. It has provided a laundry spot for many people over the years and has regularly served as an extra bedroom.

"We experimented with a variety of materials and techniques, some of which worked, some of which did not. A sealer we considered using on clay plasters on the exterior of the building failed miserably. The roof was ultra low tech, made from poles and carrizo (arrondo donax) reed, coated with several coats of clay plaster, and sealed with linseed oil, which also could have fared better. On the other hand, we tried out a variety of local clays and pigments in different paint and plaster formulas that we ultimately used throughout the various rooms of the office building.

"It has since been torn down, most of its materials recycled into an evolving cob/bamboo vault built on the original foundation by Kyle Young, our friend and bamboo aficionado."

—Athena and Bill Steen

STEENS' BIKE SHED

Canelo, Arizona

"What happens when you need to teach a plaster workshop and there is no available wall space to plaster? We constructed this little bike shed very quickly, using stabilized rammed earth for the foundation of the two independent walls. It was one of those early experiments where the value of pre-compression for increasing the lateral stability of the walls really sunk in. The walls were amazingly solid before we ever got the two walls tied together with the roof. The earthen plaster on the exterior was made with a little casein and linseed oil. It has held up remarkably well. The lime plaster on the inside was frescoed red and then painted with ferrous sulfate to get the beautiful orange-red color."

—Bill and Athena Steen

On the side shed extension, 4 x 4-inch (102 x 102-millimeter) posts were wrapped with reed mats, plastered with clay, and then sealed with linseed oil. A reed mat protects a lawn mower and weed eaters.

35

GREENHOUSES

Design guidelines for greenhouses built largely with strawbales have not been clearly established. As with any greenhouse, the trick is balancing the amount and placement of thermal mass, insulation, and glazing. There should be enough of the following:

- Glazing with good R-value glass to allow sun in to heat the space and to keep heat in the greenhouse.
- Insulation (strawbales) to retain the heat gain, allowing the thermal mass to absorb heat (strawbales are usually best placed in the east and west walls).
- Thermal mass to absorb heat and release it into the space when the sun goes down.

The interiors of greenhouses are usually warmer than the outdoors and normally more humid due to the large amount of moisture that plants transpire. Given these conditions and the fact that heat moves from warm to cold, the warm, humid air present in the greenhouse moves towards cooler areas. This can happen in a controlled manner through vents/windows or in an undesirable

Gutters used for plants in greenhouse. Canelo, Arizona.

way through leaks that result from poor air sealing. In the latter case, cooler air tries to enter through leaks in the lower half of the structure and escape through leaks in the upper half. One of the main moisture concerns can be alleviated by good air sealing that prevents warm, humid air from entering the walls. With an attached greenhouse, excess humidity will pass to the interior of a building when it is open during the day. At night, much of the humidity will condense on the glass. In the summer, the greenhouse will likely be open to the outdoors so humidity buildup shouldn't be an issue.

Indeed, greenhouses are known for condensation. Condensation occurs on all of the glass, usually at night, whether the greenhouse is equator facing or not, simply because the glass has next to no insulation. Since it can be assumed that leaks will eventually happen, it is a good idea to avoid the use of bales downstream from the inevitable condensation and/or potential leaks. If condensation gutters are not placed immediately

below the glass, repeated wetting and drying of the support framing will eventually rot the bales.

The stem wall of the greenhouse foundation should be sufficiently high so that any water that splashes or accumulates on the ground will not affect the bales. Drainage should be provided for as well. In addition, the lower courses of bales should be given a facing of a plaster, stone, or material that will resist the splash back that might occur from watering or washing plants. In particular, joints and spots where different materials meet will benefit from careful attention to prevent air leakage and insect intrusion.

A greenhouse addition to a strawbale retrofit. Rock gabion provides thermal mass while water dripping on it provides some cooling and needed humidity.

YOUTH GARDEN PROJECT GREENHOUSE

Moab, Utah

"Foundation work on the Youth Garden Project Greenhouse started in a snowstorm, but the snow didn't phase the Sterling College students. They had spent the last couple of months studying avalanches, backcountry skiing, and tourist-town economies in neighboring Colorado. We planned to build a greenhouse for the Youth Garden Project—a local nonprofit group that allows kids of all ages to work in their garden. For the Sterling students, the month-long course on sustainable building and ecological design was the last part of a multifaceted semester away from campus. The greenhouse was designed to balance the need for light and sun while providing insulation and mass for long winter nights. In the summer, insulation, interior mass, a ventilating fan, and berming would keep the interior from overheating. Plans allowed for the later addition of nighttime insulation for winter use and shading cloth for summer use, if needed.

"Earlier in the winter, we had spent a week together in the classroom, studying the principles of sustainable building. Each student then researched a component of the upcoming project in order to recommend materials to use in the building. Jason, a student from Sterling taking some time off and working with us as an intern, pulled the materials together.

A dragon relief sculpted from clay.

"We poured the simple pier footings, set juniper posts, and put up beams from the local sawmill. Jim McGann, a contractor, and the more experienced Sterling students put up the frame. My husband Kalen, between runs for needed materials, oversaw the installation of the greenhouse glazing and the 100-percent-recycled roofing material. Others focused on the earth-bag wall, which also functioned as a retaining wall to allow the building to be bermed into the ground. With the Sterling students providing the bulk of the energy, we soon started on the strawbales and then the earth plaster inside and out.

"We created a mixing pit for the plaster and mixed it with our feet. The weather had turned warm and the joys of clay, sand, straw, and water provided ample entertainment for all of us. High school students and after-school Youth Garden Project participants continued forming patios and seating areas with earth-bag walls on the two sides of the building. When it came to plaster, everyone helped. As we neared the end of the four weeks, bas relief sculptures in the plaster, inside and out, were added to complete the building.

"The Sterling students had made a great contribution to the community, learned a lot about building, and the Youth Garden now had a greenhouse. The participants finished the project by brightly painting the doors, installing shelves and irrigation, and filling the greenhouse with plants. Over the years, other groups of students have added exterior decoration, completed the patios, lime washed the interior and exterior, and planted around, on, and in the greenhouse. The Youth Garden staff have reported that the building works well not only for the plants but also as a nice place to warm up on cold winter days or escape the early morning heat in the summer."

—Susie Harrington

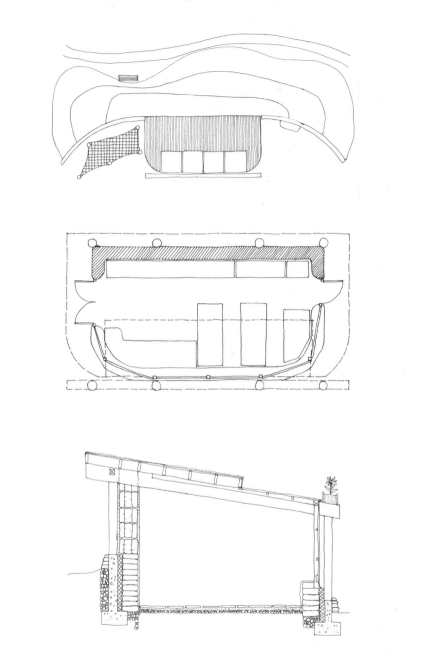

Top: The site plan for the greenhouse.

Middle: The floor plan is for a 27 x 15-1/2-foot (8.23 x 4.72-meter) exterior, with a 300-square-foot (27.88 square-meter) interior.

Bottom: Section of the greenhouse.

SUNROOMS

The addition of a sunspace onto the equator-facing side of the building dramatically affects the heating and cooling of a house. It insulates the house against extreme temperature changes. In winter, it absorbs the heat from the sun and heats the house and yet is isolated from the house during the nights when outside temperatures start to drop. During the summer, the sunspace can remain closed to the house or can be transformed into a screened area. Because sunrooms are auxiliary buffer zones rather than conditioned living spaces (using no energy to heat and cool), inexpensive or recycled glazing can be used since it is much less critical if they are leaky and poorly insulated.

Using vertical glazing on the walls with an opaque roof makes it easier to control the amount of solar gain, especially in summer when gains through unshaded overhead glazing can cause the space to overheat and in winter when heat can be lost through uninsulated overhead glazing during non-gain periods.

Besides acting as a heater, sunrooms are transitional spaces that can serve a multitude of purposes. Housed with plants, sunrooms can generate additional humidity, which in arid climates is especially beneficial. Plants in pots that are frost sensitive can be stored in the sunrooms during winters and moved outside for the summer. Sunrooms make great places to dry clothes or food, or to just sit and bask in the warm winter sun.

Sunspace off of Bill and Nancy Cook's rammed-earth house. Sonoita, Arizona.

ENERGY EFFICIENCY & NATURAL CONDITIONING

Highly insulated strawbale walls can be used as part of a house or building to ensure it remains comfortable throughout most of the year with very little supplemental heating and cooling. However, the walls by themselves are not sufficient for that goal to be achieved. An overall strategy is needed for highly efficient performance. The strategy must incorporate the following elements:

- Insulation for the foundation, roof, rim joists, windows, and doors that complement the walls.
- Air-sealing measures that control energy loss and moisture flows (infiltration and exfiltration leaks can account for up to 50 percent of the heat loss).
- A building site and orientation that allows for passive heating and cooling.
- Thermal mass provided by the interior plaster in conjunction with a masonry floor that enables the building to "ride" through an extended cold, sunless period (any more than this is generally considered to be "lazy mass" and contributes very little to moderating diurnal temperature swings).

- Shading that prevents unwanted solar gains (a consideration that is too often overlooked but that is very helpful in keeping the building cool in summer).
- Site planning, improvements, and landscaping that ensure good performance (vegetation, walls, fences, and other buildings can be utilized to break the wind, directing breezes to provide cooling and shading).

South window with lime plaster and casein paint. Canelo, Arizona.

LOGAN HIGH SCHOOL GREENHOUSE

Logan, Utah

"School-budget cutbacks nixed our original greenhouse plans. However, with the help of Wayne Bingham, we decided to build something simpler out of strawbales.

"I realized a dream could become a reality with a bit of luck, the help of a few dedicated individuals, local materials from the building site, and salvaged materials from the neighborhood. The greenhouse grew out of the place it was located. The super insulation offered by the strawbale walls, thermal mass in the floor and back wall, and solar gain were a magic combination. Since then I've added a small, temporary brick trombe wall and four fifty-gallon barrels of water for additional thermal mass. The winter following its completion was brutally cold (twenty to thirty below zero at night and well below zero in the day), and this building never dropped below twenty-five degrees Fahrenheit! This was totally unexpected, since it was off the grid and it had no internal source of heat. If I were to do it again, I would put an overhang on the front of the roof to protect the earthen plaster from moisture. (I would also make it large enough so that I could move in!) Beyond this, the building is highly functional and very attractive.

"We were very fortunate to have a donated source of salvaged wood located less than a block from our project. Along with this, many local businesses gave us discount rates, and some made outright donations of materials. We purchased our wheat straw from a local farm for sixty cents a bale—a great buy! At first, sand and gravel were donated to us, and then we purchased it at discounted prices. We had free access to a local construction site with heavy clay soil. We used the clay for earth plaster. The Kalwall double-glazed windows were salvaged from a school that was in the process of replacing them with upgraded windows. The

Exterior dimensions are 20 x 12 feet (6.10 x 3.66 meters), for 240 square feet (22.32 square meters). Interior dimensions are 17 x 9.5 feet (5.18 x 2.90 meters), for 161 square feet (14.96 square meters).

total dollar cost of our building materials was about $2,000.

"The aesthetic appeal of this building is quite extraordinary. My students marvel at its warmth and ambiance. They just like to hang out in and around the building to feel its presence. None had seen such a building before and frequently commented that they would love to have a house like it someday. The tawny gold colored, thick walls with rounded, somewhat undulating corners; vintage, multicolored brick floor; and natural lighting all add to its allure.

"The color for the reddish brown trim was manufactured on-site from a natural iron oxide material originating from a cave in France, supposedly the same cave and formulation used by Michelangelo. The wall color was achieved as a result of chemical reaction between the calcium carbonate in the lime plaster and a ferrous sulfate wash.

"Teachers, students, and neighbors have all utilized the greenhouse's space for everything from starting tomatoes to growing native seedlings to be used for water-efficient landscaping on the school grounds. We now have an organic garden next to the greenhouse. We use a rainwater harvest system from the greenhouse roof as our main source of water both in and out of the greenhouse."

—Jack Greene

COLORADO ROCKY MOUNTAIN SCHOOL GREENHOUSE

Carbondale, Colorado

"Most institutions have at least one individual who is always looking to try something new. At Colorado Rocky Mountain School (CRMS) in Carbondale, Colorado, Tim Taylor, a young math teacher, wanted to build a strawbale structure. At the same time, the garden program needed a potting shed. The idea and the need were combined, and students and parents joined together to make the strawbale building at CRMS a reality.

"After securing funding from the BKS Family Foundation and the help of a local architect to design the structure, a group of parent volunteers gathered together on a 16-degree day in December to erect the post and beam structure that would support the roof. Students had earlier dug the holes and poured the footers. In March, during interim, a one-week period when students and teachers leave the traditional classroom behind to focus on a hands-on learning experience, students and faculty stacked the bales and applied the first coat of stucco. The remainder of the work was completed over the course of a year by student work crews.

"The CRMS strawbale potting shed was built for $11,000 in materials. With a little under 350 square feet (32.5 square meters) of interior space, the building is small but very functional. One of its best features is the glass garage door that when opened blurs the boundary between the indoors and outdoors. There is an additional 120 square feet (11.15 square meters) of storage for tools and supplies that is accessed from the back of the building. Though the structure has no supplemental heat, the temperature never drops below forty or fifty degrees even on the coldest days. Students work through the winter, starting plants from seed and cuttings for use in the garden in the spring. The building has functioned without any problems for over five years and is still going strong."

—Linda Halloran

47

CANELO PROJECT OUTBUILDINGS

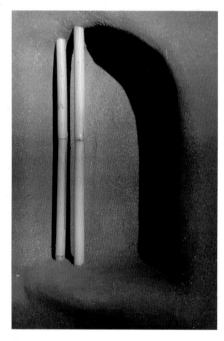

Earth-plastered niche with exposed bamboo pin and disguised all-thread tie down. Canelo, Arizona.

"Most people need a storage building, shop, pump house, or some other type of accessory building, and we are not exceptions. By constructing a number of small shop and storage buildings instead of one large one, we've been able to accommodate our changing needs while experimenting with different materials and techniques. Keeping the scale of things small has prevented errors from being catastrophic. Since our risks were calculated, any adjustments and changes needed, though frustrating, were not impossible.

"Much of what we do revolves around the myriad of ways clay can be combined with straw and other natural fibers when used in plasters, floors, and built-in furniture. To round out our palette of natural materials, we also use a little lime, casein, starches, and assorted pigments.

"We have been influenced by clay and lime work from Japan, Germany, and England, but our work in Mexico impacted us the most. Many of the techniques we use originated there while working with poor families. We were forced to see the world through their eyes and use tools and materials in ways that were within their financial reach. The lack of mechanization brought a different kind of elegance and dignity to the work we did together and consequently taught us to put a higher value on the work people did rather than machines.

"We became conscious of how easily priorities get blurred when modern tools and materials are involved. Buildings are constructed more quickly and get bigger and bigger, using more and more energy and materials in the process. Simultaneously buildings often lack many aesthetic qualities.

"Little strawbale structures, rich with personality, have taught us so many things, but perhaps most importantly, they have taught us how

Participants apply a clay slip directly on the bale walls during a Canelo Project workshop.

much more interesting and beautiful building can be when structures are largely handcrafted and small, and the doors of participation are left open for the process to be graced with heart and soul."

—Bill and Athena Steen
The Canelo Project
www.caneloproject.com

49

PUMP HOUSE

The original pump house was the only building that burned during a 50,000-acre fire in 2002. This new pump house was completed during a weeklong, comprehensive strawbale workshop.

The east wall is made of clay-lime. The lime makes the clay weather resistant.

The interior walls and pressure tank were finished with wheat paste and clay paint.

Top: Wall textured with holes to key a future coat of lime plaster.

Bottom: Clay-lime plaster.

Opposite and above: A clay-straw plaster stabilized with casein and linseed oil. The little pent roof, made from local bear grass, conveys the feeling of thatch without covering the entire building.

BOTTLE WINDOWS

An excellent way to recycle glass bottles is to use them as windows, much like glass blocks. Bottles allow light to shine through without loss of privacy. Just about any bottle or combination of bottles will work. Filling them with broken glass, marbles, or other semitransparent materials will make them even more interesting. When you use colored bottles, you get colored light. The variations of pattern, light, color, and texture are limited only by your imagination.

There is no established method for installing bottles in a wall, but they are easiest set into walls that are plastered with clay. For starters, the bottles need to be thoroughly cleaned and dried before sealing them with the original cap, cork, or duct tape. Each is placed into an opening slightly larger than the bottle and sculpted in with a mix of clay and straw. Bottles should be placed on something like a neoprene block. When working the clay around the bottles, it is best to leave some space above and around them so that if any pressure is exerted upon them, there will be some give to help avert breakage. Caulk or a finer clay and sand mixture can be used to seal the joints between two or more adjoining bottles.

This is the kind of work that one should approach with the idea that someday one or more of the bottles will break and need to be replaced. Obviously this is not fun, but it is not particularly difficult to fix. It is ideal if one creates a slightly different molding around each bottle, changing the color or using any other detail or method that avoids matching the original finish.

Workshop participants set recycled glass bottles into a mortar bed of cob.

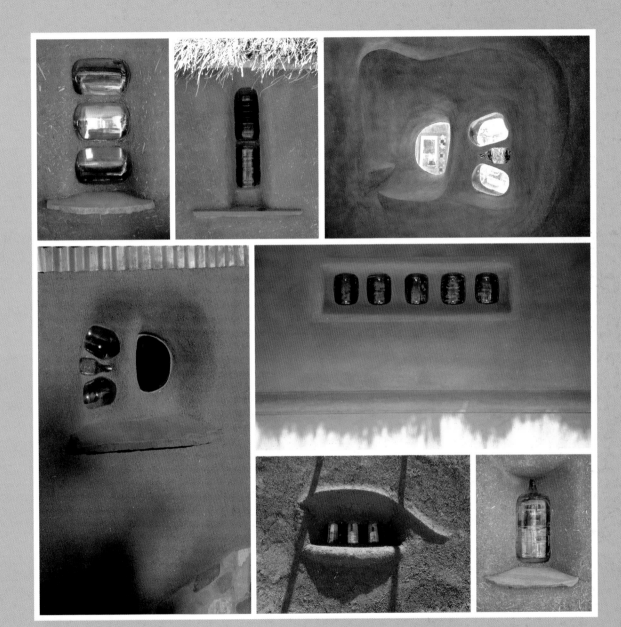

53

BUCKET SHED

The bucket shed was built to store the raw materials used in plasters—clay, lime, and assorted aggregates. Dry materials are stored under the porch where the plastic buckets are protected from the weather. Clay and lime putties are kept inside to avoid freezing. A variety of plaster surfaces adorn the little building. The door is plywood covered with diagonal pieces of bamboo and reed mats.

Top, left and right: A thin wall of reed mats woven around small diameter poles is plastered on both sides with a straw-clay mix. The outer layer of the exterior plaster contains a small amount of lime. The wall could make an interesting interior partition.

Left: Two of the interior walls are lime plastered and frescoed with a light blue. The end walls have a gray sand finish that uses wheat paste as a binder. The shelves were painted with colorful stains that used beer as the binder.

The blue wall is lime-plastered and frescoed with an ultramarine blue Mexican pigment called azul anil. *Along the outer edges, the white lime was carved away to expose the clay plaster beneath.*

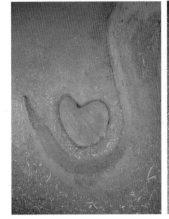
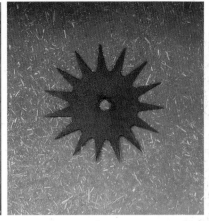

BLUEWALL PAINT SHED

Built on a foundation of recycled concrete pieces, this load-bearing building is used to store paint, plaster materials, and tools. Over the years, it has become an informal mini research lab that has been at the heart of many experimental wall finishes and sample test boards.

One-coat straw-clay plaster mix finished to expose the straw.

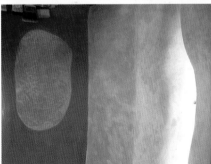

Bottom, left: The brown plaster is polished clay-lime. The center portion is a sample of a Moroccan-polished lime plaster sealed with olive oil soap, known as tadelakt. The blue-green plaster on the right is lime frescoed with copper sulfate and yellow oxide.

57

MANDALA SHED

The mandala shed is one of the most highly decorated storage buildings anyone is likely to encounter. Its uneven lines and homemade finishes convey a feeling of antiquity and character.

The metal corrugated roofing was colored with ferric nitrate to achieve its rusty color.

Left: A lime-plastered niche.

Right: The arched opening was formed using split green bamboo. The counter and shelves were built with straw-clay blocks and plastered with clay-lime sealed with olive oil soap. The design above the counter was created with a stencil pressed into moist clay plaster. The floor is shale and clay sealed with linseed oil.

CARVED MURALS

Beautiful murals can be created by carving away layers of plaster to reveal different colored or textured layers beneath. Contrast between the layers can be achieved by using different colored clays or a different plaster material such as lime or clay-lime.

Even simple carvings can have a striking effect. Straight-line designs are easier for beginners to cut than ones with curves. Timing is ever so important since the top plaster coat carves best when it is leather hard, which usually happens a couple of hours after being applied.

Color can also be achieved by using "fresco," or painting the lime or clay-lime plaster while it is still damp. Once again, timing is everything. The color will not fuse with the plaster if it has dried out. It is also best not to burnish the plaster first because it restricts its ability to absorb the pigment.

Colors can be added later by using any number of different paints. Starch and casein paints are good for interior surfaces while silicate (water-glass) paints work well for masonry surfaces that are exposed to weather.

Minor carving to clean the edges and details can be done during the next couple of days. Inlays of other colored plasters can also be done later. A basic knife works well to

first score then cut the edges at a 45-degree angle away from the area to be carved. Any flat-edge tool, such as a putty knife or five-in-one tool, works to scrape away the plaster.

Athena carves the lime plaster away to expose the clay-sand layer beneath.

61

WOOD SHED

The wood shed has a small work area and tool storage on the interior with additional workspace and storage under the porches. The stem wall of the foundation is built of concrete block that is finished with a cement stucco to resemble blocks of stone.

The interior bale walls, unfinished at the time of this photo, have been coated with a base coat of thick straw-clay. Bamboo poles form the arch, the remaining cavity to be filled with cellulose and closed with a moldable mix of clay and straw.

A stencil pressed into moist clay plaster defines where two different plasters meet. The windowsill is made from acid-stained cement stucco over wood.

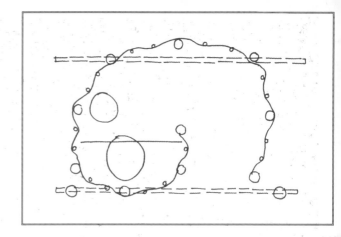

SAWDUST TOILET

"Like many others, we spent years searching for a simple, inexpensive, and effective way of dealing with human waste. It can become a complicated and/or expensive endeavor as a result of the sheer complexity and difficulty of designing and installing conventional systems. For us, and many others, the sawdust toilet is an effective solution.

"The sawdust toilet consists of little more than a five-gallon bucket, a toilet seat, an enclosure for the bucket (not necessary) and a supply of sawdust, peat moss, shredded junk mail, leaves, etc. After each use, a handful or two of sawdust is thrown in. Once full, the bucket is emptied into a compost bin. After thoroughly composted, this can be used to improve poor soils. We use it to fertilize our bamboo groves and fruit trees.

"Unlike the outhouse, the sawdust toilet is movable and a lot easier to set up (no hole to dig). It is odorless, free of flies, and doesn't pollute water supplies. Unlike most more expensive composting toilets, there are no moving parts, and it doesn't require electricity. Furthermore, it doesn't unnecessarily waste precious water supplies like the common flush toilet. It can be simply made or it can be adorned and decorated with a more elegant enclosure built to house the bucket.

"Our sawdust toilet sits in the shade of a large oak tree with a little window that looks out on newly planted bamboo. It's housed in a spiral enclosure made from juniper poles, reeds, and clay. It's the perfect place to listen to the chirping of the insects, the songs of the birds, or the softly falling rain.

"The definitive book on this subject is *The Humanure Handbook* by Joseph Jenkins available at www.jenkinspublishing.com. Not only informative, it is extremely good and fun reading."

—Bill and Athena Steen

A spiral floor plan provides privacy for toilets or showers.

65

TINY STUDIOS & MEDITATION RETREATS

An altar niche in Mary Rosa's strawbale studio. Sahuarita, Arizona.

Not quite houses, these one-room structures are the kind of places that linger in the imagination—places where one can escape the chaos and challenges of everyday life to dream or rest. They vary in shape and form—from studios to retreats, meditation spaces, huts, and offices—depending on the needs of the imaginer. They are places of peace and solitude where one might cultivate oneself or one's work.

Worthy works written by others sharing the same fascination for smaller places include *Walden* by Henry David Thoreau, *A Room of One's Own* by Virginia Woolf, *A Pattern Language* by Christopher Alexander, *The Tiny Book of Tiny Houses* by Lester Walker, *Retreats* by Lawson Drinkard III, *Poetics of Space* by Gaston Bachelard, and *A Place of My Own* by Michael Pollan. And although difficult to find, there is a beautiful book written by a Japanese man who had reduced his life to 100 square feet (9.30 square meters). We wish we knew the name of the book.

These are spaces that spring from the dreams and hands of the person who builds and uses them. They provide a perfect opportunity to make vague images as tangible and real as they are personal and unique. Since the scale is small, these structures can be effective in tempting someone who has never built before into taking their first steps into the world of building. And perhaps it is with good reason that little structures of this type lack the complexity of larger places with bathrooms, kitchens, and code requirements.

Floor plans can be inventive yet simple and straightforward. Potential mistakes are minor considerations, especially when compared with the pitfalls and surprises that are possible when constructing the larger dream house. Attempts to translate one's lifetime of expectations and fantasies into built form rarely mesh with the realities of budget and what it takes to actually get something built. It is best to build your dream home on a small, delightful, and manageable scale.

Carol Anthony's teensy meditation hut thatched with local flower stalks and plastered with earth. Santa Fe, New Mexico.

CAROL'S CLOISTER

Santa Fe, New Mexico

"I built my cloister with friends, some great humor, tequila, and, now and then, hugs, money, and delicious ratatouille. For me, straw, mud, and sunshine all equal pure religion. The land, sky, and the feel of people working together with their hands and hearts all add up to that brand of life experience that nourishes the soul for years to come.

"My cloister overlooks the clear meadow of the Twin Mountain Peaks. This slice of land with its sand, rock, chamisa, and juniper is a piece of the eighteenth century frozen in time. The land honors and protects the gardens and planted trees within the strawbale walls.

"All is aligned to that particular mountain view and viewpoint of spirit. Here my dreams and thoughts are written, drawn, and grounded. I become still and listen. This cloister is my version and vision of remembered inner courtyards and atriums of Italian Pompeian and Herculaneum villas. Energy and mystery play an integral part here. The strawbales not only define the thickness, strength, and curves of the walls, but also lend an old-fashioned aesthetic warmth and early southwestern architectural feel. The cloister—my house, studio, and sanctuary—is a soulful dance finally realized."

—Carol Anthony

The strawbale addition onto an existing house.

Opposite, upper left: A sculpted straw-clay arch over the door creates an inviting entryway.

Opposite, lower left: A strawbale window seat. The window lintel is made from yucca stalks.

Opposite, right: A plastered strawbale wall on a stone foundation defines the entrance.

Carol's pear painting with two stones
for her and her twin sister.

Left: The bale walls were sculpted
with straw-clay plasters, and then
painted with clay and wheat-paste
paint.

ACCESSORY STRUCTURES EXEMPT FROM BUILDING PERMITS

by Matts Myhrman of Out On Bale

In the past it was possible to legally build small, nonresidential structures without benefit of code (i.e., without a permit) only if:

1) you were building on land controlled by entities that have their own rules (e.g., universities, Indian reservations, etc.)

2) you were building an agricultural building that was exempt from permitting

3) you were keeping the "hatprint" of the building below a given square footage. The "hatprint" is the area of the roof projected down onto a horizontal plane (imagine hanging a plumb bob from each corner of the roof to the ground, drawing lines between the points where the plumb bob hits, and calculating the area within these lines). For any building site within entities using the Uniform Building Code (UBC)—i.e., in most of the western United States—the "hatprint" could not exceed 120 square feet (10 x 12 feet or 3.05 x 3.66 meters).

Since most people want to build a small, nonagricultural, nonresidential structure for their own use themselves, or have it built for them, the 120-square-foot (11.50-square-meter) "hatprint" has been the code sphincter through which their structure has had to pass.

A block foundation ready for bales. The sill plates are filled with gravel to ensure good drainage beneath the bales.

As thick-wall enthusiasts, we have had to build our thick walls within the prescribed "hatprint," a requirement that patently discriminates against the use of the natural building systems that we hold so dear. But wait, dear friends, don't end it all by jumping off that bale stack into a sticky pit of cob. A glimmer of hope appears over the regulatory horizon, tucked away within the new International Residential Code (IRC) for One and Two Family Dwellings, 2000. I thank David Eisenberg of DCAT for alerting me to it. The IRC, 2000, is a new residential building code intended to replace the several different building codes traditionally used within the country. Jurisdictions (states, counties, and cities) are in various stages of replacing their previously adopted code with this new code. The key, for us, lies in Section R105.2 of Chapter 1, Part 1, which reads as follows:

R105.2 Work exempt from permit. Permits shall not be required for the following. Exemption from the permit requirements of this code shall not be deemed to grant authorization for any work to be done in any manner in violation of the provisions of this code or any other laws or ordinances of this jurisdiction.

Building:
1. One story detached accessory structures, provided the floor area does not exceed 200 square feet (18.58 square meters).

The beauty of this is that it prescribes a maximum allowed floor area of 200 square feet, outside of which walls of any thickness may be built. To learn what the IRC means by an "accessory structure," we must go to Chapter 2, Part 11, Section R202, where we find:

ACCESSORY STRUCTURE. In one- and two-family dwellings not more than three stories high with separate means of egress, a building, the use of which is incidental to that of the main building and which is located on the same lot.

Finally, to learn what the IRC means by "floor area," although we might think this obvious, we must go to a different code, the International Building Code (IBC), 2000. In Chapter 2, Section 202, we find "Floor Area, Gross," but are further referred to Section 1002.1, where we find

Bale walls are stacked in a running bond and sewn together at the corners.

Chapter 10 of the IBC, 2000. There we find the following definition:

FLOOR AREA, GROSS. The floor area within the inside perimeter of the exterior walls of the building under consideration, exclusive of vent shafts and courts, without deduction for corridors, stairways, closets, the thickness of interior walls, columns or other features.

This definition makes it clear that any portion of a floor deck or slab on which the exterior walls sit is not to be considered part of the floor area. The floor area is therefore determined by the interior dimensions of the structure, not the exterior dimensions.

These various sections from the IRC and IBC, taken together, provide the basis for legally building a permit-exempt accessory building with a floor area not exceeding 200 square feet (18.59 square meters). This could be a rectangular floor area 10 x 20 (3.05 x 6.10 meters), a square floor area of about 14 feet one inch (4.29 meters) per side, or a circular floor area with a diameter of just under 16 feet (4.88 meters). Compared with what was possible under the UBC, if using a thick-walled system, this is palatial. So, go for it, while remembering to also comply with any applicable zoning considerations (e.g., distance from other structures, setbacks from lot lines, etc.).

A flat-roof truss for the gable end is going on top of a load-bearing bale structure.

WINDOW SEATS

Everyone loves a window seat. Instinctively we are drawn to the natural light. With book in hand and a cup of tea, we are ready to nestle in alone and drift for a few moments out into the expansive view of snow falling on a winter's day.

Window seats are usually best suited to one reclining person, perhaps two. Ideally they should be long enough for a person to lie down, but a shorter seat will also work. Window seats should be about the thickness of three string bale walls. The practical minimum width for any seating is about 18 inches (457.20 millimeters) with 2 feet (609.60 millimeters) even better. Bumping out the wall at windows by a bale width may be an alternative for two-string bales or bales on edge if stealing floor space from the interior to create the generous window seat is not desirable. The bump out would also help stabilize the wall, effectively creating a buttress or pilaster on either side of the opening.

One bale height below the window with a few cushions is just about right. Add a few pillows, a cushion, and mattress and it's done. For sleeping, the seat can be widened to make room for a single or even a double mattress by either extending the seat frame to the interior or protruding the entire window to the exterior. To increase efficiency, storage could also be incorporated beneath the seat or bed.

A window seat within the thick strawbale walls. Santa Sabino, California.

SUSIE'S GARDEN OFFICE

Moab, Utah

"Having my office in our bedroom wasn't working. The singlewide trailer that was our home was not absorbing another function gracefully. I looked around town for a place to rent. It was a hard to find any space I wanted to work in, and the added drawback of $250 per month for rent (if I got at least one window) spurred me towards other solutions. My design business was taking a lot of time, and I really didn't need another project; but nothing else made sense, so I decided to build a small studio. Fortunately, three friends were around with whom I had worked on other projects: Miguel, who had done quite a bit of natural building; Melissa, who wanted more building experience; and Kevin, whose can-do attitude made up for his lack of experience and knowledge.

"I was too busy drawing other people's plans to bother with drawing my own, so a sketch had to do. We began in March with the rental of a Bobcat. Starting with a flattened area, we hand dug holes for six small footers and a gravel trench foundation. Six locally harvested junipers and three glulams reclaimed from an old building provided the structure. The roof was made of I-joists, plywood sheathing, and a waterproof membrane.

"With our friends Kaki and Donny, we put down a couple of courses of earth bags to support the strawbales. After anchoring the window and door bucks into the foundation, we put up the straw.

"Days were getting warmer. Kevin had moved on to other projects, but Melissa and

Opposite: The exterior lime plaster was colored with a red oxide. Keeping the structural posts separate from the bale walls made plastering and finishing details easier.

77

Miguel kept going. As I got pulled back into my work, Melissa and Miguel plastered the inside and outside with hand-mixed (and foot-mixed) earth plaster. We finished the interior with a local white clay and yellow ochre wash. The cob seat took many batches, but the adobe floor went fast.

"We ran the exterior plaster all the way to the ground to hide the earth bags—a mistake we still need to fix. We finished the exterior with troweled lime, fresco applied after for color. The lime has shelled off in some places, and needs repair. It was more tempermental than we expected.

"Sometime early on we decided to make a living roof. I had been interested in learning more about what would work in our climate, and experimenting on a small place seemed like a good plan. Although highly refined systems for living roofs are available, they're all a little pricey for a backyard project, so we just went with a layer of straw and some dirt. We had to run irrigation to the roof, which admittedly seems a little strange, otherwise not much would grow in our arid climate. The first year we planted a lot of plants, a few of which survived. After that, we let it plant itself. I weeded the tamarisk, cottonwood seedlings, and sandburs, and then hoped for the best. Eventually grasses took over. It wasn't the cascade of flowers I had originally envisioned, but it was satisfying enough.

"In May, I moved in, set up shop, and kept working. In the summer, a fan helped cool the building at night, and it stayed cool during the day; in the winter, the large south windows kept it light and warm (we did put in a small propane heater eventually). We delighted in both the small native garden we planted around the new studio and in the view of the vegetable garden and red cliffs beyond.

"The office served me well. When we moved after five years, I was happy to leave the trailer, but sad to leave the little studio. I rebuilt almost the exact same studio, with a few improvements, in a new location."

—Susie Harrington
Gaia Design
www.withgaia.org

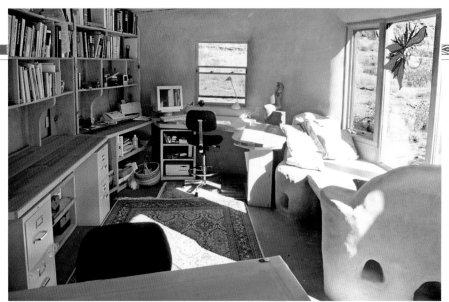

A non-rectangular floor plan. Dimensions are 24 x 19 feet (7.32 x 5.79 meters). Interior square footage is roughly 300 square feet (27.87 square meters).

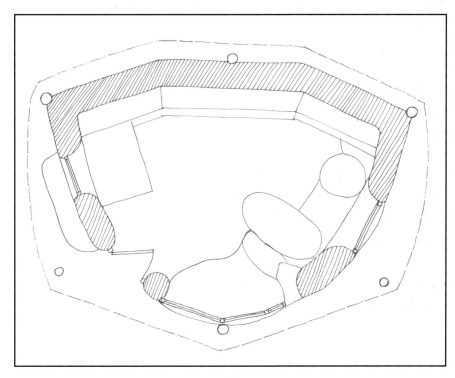

THE "PIE": JOHN'S MEDITATION CABIN

Northern California

"My wife, Prema, and I have practiced meditation for many years, and we know that committed spiritual practitioners often need a place for long-term solitary retreat, a place that's quiet and undisturbed, but with friends nearby to offer support for basic needs like food shopping. We decided to build one or two small hermitages and make them available for people to use for months or years of retreat. With pure motivation, we knew this would be an offering not just to the 'hermit,' but also to the land, the creatures, the entire community, and the world.

"Little buildings are fun to design since one simple concept can be carried out without conflict. The location of this cabin is quiet and peaceful, and we wanted a stable, grounded building to complement the site. We chose a round shape that would be partially dug into the hillside. The building is 12 feet (3.66 meters) in diameter inside, with a kitchen and closet fit into the 2-foot (.61-meter) bale walls. Since one person will live inside all day long, every day, we wanted this small room to feel large and expansive, so we made a high ceiling that 'floats' above the bale walls on a ring of clerestory windows. The abundant natural light also means that electric lights are needed only at night. The site is the sunniest spot on our property and could be unbearable in the heat of summer. To protect the roof from sun and also blend the building with the landscape, we decided on a living roof. The soil is watered each morning, and the damp soil absorbs, evaporates, and stores much of the sun's heat and gives it back to the night sky without it ever entering the insulation envelope.

The interior with an altar. The strip of windows floods light in without loss of privacy.

Opposite: The exterior cement stucco was colored with ferrous sulfate and red iron oxide while the plaster was curing. Clear panels extend out to protect the door but do not cut out light.

81

The exterior cement stucco was colored with ferrous sulfate and red iron oxide while the plaster was curing. Clear panels extend out to protect the door but do not cut out light.

"Naturally, we wanted the building to be healthy, so we used natural and non-toxic materials: lime plaster, earthen floor, casein paints, mineral pigments, concrete windowsills, and countertops. We had some friends over to dedicate the building the day it was finished, and it was wonderful to sit inside and feel good about breathing the air—the building smelled wonderful!"

—John Swearingen
www.skillful-means.com

82

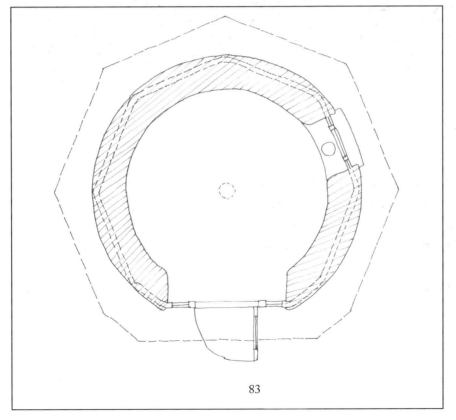

Built in a seismically active area, the structure supports the roof while the bale walls wrapped in wire mesh provide strength. Built in the style of a yurt, the main beams press against a 12-inch steel pipe at the center and are restrained on the outside by a cable. The interior and exterior surfaces of the walls are covered with hydraulic lime plaster. Two shades of raw sienna pigment give color to the outside. Every effort was made to eliminate toxic materials from the building. The roof was constructed of two layers of Bituthene, a plastic waffle drainage layer/membrane protector, and five inches of lightweight earth mix. Perforated plastic drain pipe is wrapped around the roof edge to restrain the earth while allowing drainage.

83

RAYMOND'S STUDIO

Village of Dunning, Scotland

"Raymond and Jean Young came to us wanting to build a small office. I was working for Gaia Architects at the time. The Youngs had two definites—round poles and a roof that grew strawberries. Beyond that, they were open to persuasion and to using the project as an experiment. Initially, they kept drawing the walls very thick, very much like primitive, sheltering elements, and this made me think of strawbales because they are very basic, thick, and provide sheltering as well as a warm sort of simplicity and symbolism. The Youngs eagerly shared our enthusiasm for modern design, with a sympathy for natural materials and traditional techniques.

"The building was kept under the limit for building warrant, so we could speed up the process of getting on site. Our friend Charles Dobb was the builder who took on the job with equal enthusiasm and dedication. He handcrafted the laminated, curved beams that hold up the roof.

"The building was erected for about £16,000 in 1999. It is only 28 square meters (301.39 square feet) in total. To try to increase the apparent size, I cut out two corners to create a welcoming entrance area and a balcony facing the garden. This decreased the actual size, but increased the feeling of space as there are now three overall spaces. The more interesting internal space also helps reduce the sense of it being really only a wee room.

"We used a leftover section of gas main pipe for a window—in the United Kingdom, the diameter is exactly the same dimension as a bale height so it was a lintel-less window, which was something I wanted. All the associated boxing around the walls is either completely straw or completely glazed. This fact simplified and sped up the process a lot.

"We applied the first-ever 'breathing base' to the walls. I was convinced from reading about the buildup of moisture at the outer base of walls that the base of the wall itself should also be moisture transfusive. The bales sit on woodwool (insulating board made from wood shavings) over floorboards with gaps between so there cannot be any potentially harmful buildup of moisture.

"We also used yachting cables to brace the structure, which cost a lot, and sheep wool from a textile mill for the floor and roof insulation. The commercial sheep wool was about twenty times the price of mineral wool at the time (now it is only five times) so the only way we could afford it was to cheat and get sub-textile grade stuff from the mills in Bradford.

"What I like most is that, so far, this studio is the only building that I have designed completely myself, from scratch, and it turned out how I had hoped. I like how it is both modern, yet wholly ecological, using only natural or recycled, locally sourced, and completely non-toxic materials. It was one of those projects where all the right people did their best, and it worked really well.

"Some people say it is a bit too 'cute,' due, I think, to the curved roof and wobbly walls. After attempting to fill in all the irregularities, we asked ourselves why we were pretending these were normal flat walls. We stopped filling and left them as they were. The structure is quite minimalist and not at all sentimental."

—Chris Morgan
Locate Architects
www.locatearchitects.co.uk

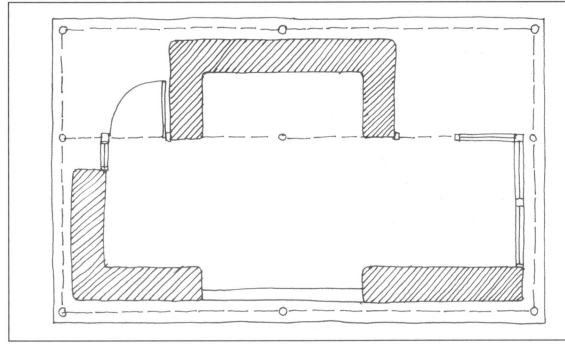

*Floor plan is
28 square meters
(301.39 square
feet).*

THE SHED ROOF

Plain, simple, and often inconspicuous, the shed roof is about the easiest roof to build and, therefore, a good project for the inexperienced builder. A parallel layout of the rafters or trusses, which requires only simple math, and a framing square are required.

As the width of a building increases, the distance that a rafter needs to span may exceed the capacity of readily available, solid-lumber members.

This necessitates the use of intermediate carrying beams or bearing partitions to shorten the rafter spans, or, if column-free, partition-free interiors are desired, the use of trusses or engineered lumber.

Shed roofs are usually built with a minimal difference in height between the walls upon which the ends of the rafters sit. Then, if additional intermediate floor levels, like lofts or mezzanines

are desired, the height of one or both of the end-bearing walls can be increased, or you can build "pop outs" in the roof to accommodate those spaces.

In areas of high wind, rain, and snowfall, a roof with a greater slope is usually preferable. In snow country, if the building is exposed to winds, low-slope roofs may be okay since the winds tend to keep the roof swept clean of snow. On the other hand, if the building is in a sheltered area, the snow could accumulate to the point of roof collapse.

There are several ways that strawbale walls have been used with shed roofs. What might seem like the most obvious and easiest way is probably the least desirable and troublesome, and is probably not allowable by code. One wall is built higher with a separate roof plate or beam used on the front and back walls and rafters used to connect the two. Unfortunately, this makes it extremely difficult to create the continuous top

Top: The four bale walls are connected with a plate. A built-up pony wall gives the extra height needed for the slope of the shed roof.

Bottom: The bale walls remain of equal height, and the truss determines the slope.

plate necessary to connect and stiffen the tops of the walls. A far better and stronger method is to build all walls the same height and connect them with a roof plate or beam. A pony wall (a short insulated frame wall on the roof plate) with rafters or shed roof trusses for more insulation can be used to achieve the slope of the roof.

89

JOHN & JEANNE'S MUSIC HOUSE

Tucson, Arizona

John Ronstadt and Jeanne Kresser.

Opposite: The interior functions as a music studio, computer office, and guest bedroom. Dimensions are 12 x 21 feet (3.66 x 6.40 meters). Interior is 162 square feet (15.06 square meters).

"The irony is that I come from a place where there was no accountability for what I used, where I used it, and where I disposed of it because that's the way people did it all around me. To realize that everything is living and not separate from us is something I had to discover on my own. It took me a quarter or better of a century to disconnect from all the ongoing processes around me. So many things were part of that process. Many things invisible at first became obvious with the passage of time. They have all been part of what was a jumpstart into discovering in myself what feels right.

"While we built the strawbale foundation of the house, I rebuilt my own. When I smoothed the plaster over walls that curve, I noticed and appreciated the sensuality of my own body and others' bodies. The straw poked awareness in me of textures I can bring into other parts of my life. Colors that I stirred in paint seemed to appear everywhere. I got curious about what would happen if I poured cochineal or prickly pear juice into a clay paint, and then I got excited about my curiosity. It charged me up with a vitality that rose to a level that invited matching energies to come visit.

"I feel alive in this studio. Small wonder that everything it took to build it, from the community of friends and helpers to the materials from which it is made, is alive. The strawbale is luminous and transcendent in its impermanence. It is no wonder light loves playing in every nook and cranny of our handmade home."

—Jeanne Kresser

BILL & ATHENA'S
GUEST ROOM

A niche painted with clay, mica, and wheat paste.

Canelo, Arizona

"The first strawbale house we built together very much embodies the story of our continuing saga here at our home in Canelo, a hundred-year-old homestead in southeastern Arizona tucked along a cottonwood-lined creek. It's our home, the place we work, and for all practical purposes it is the center of our lives. As fulfilling as it has been to live here, it has been equally difficult, at times sending us into depths of the unknown. It is a pure blessing that we continue to live here.

"It was 1990 and one or our early struggles was to finalize a divorce settlement between Bill and his first wife. She wanted her share of the property immediately—our time was running out. Since we had no resources to speak of, the only option might be to sell the place. We did not want to do this, so we were stuck in limbo. For us, there was no worse feeling. One morning, tired of the frustration and wear of not knowing, living like victims, we looked at each other and decided the only thing we could do was just act as if we were going to be able to stay there. The most definitive demonstration of intent we could think of was to build something.

93

"So in that spirit we designed a small strawbale passive-solar guest room with bath. It was to be the first Canelo Project workshop and the first strawbale workshop that we know of. We had no spare funds with which to build so we worked hard and got most of the materials donated. It was an amazing weeklong event that brought together Matts Myhrman, Judy Knox, and David Bainbridge, along with Steve and Carol Escott, Paul Weiner, Sue Mullen, a number of whom have gone on to become instrumental strawbale builders and teachers. And of course, throughout the week, people and realtors continued to parade through to look at the land. Talk about two levels of reality coexisting.

"We often think about what that building started and what would have happened had we not taken that leap of faith. Had we given into fear and not trusted the place and the unknown, our future would have been a lot different and perhaps a lot less fulfilling. It's both amazing and amusing to think that in many ways our lives haven't changed much since those early days and yet everything is totally different. The one constant is that our trust continues to grow both in the place and in each other.

"As for the building itself, there's not a whole lot to say. It's a hybrid structure, load-bearing on the back wall, with a frame wall on the front south wall. The interior adobe partition wall provides thermal mass and a seat, and it divides the bathroom from the living area. Even though the building is nothing more than a simple rectangle, the curved wall creates the feeling of a very different kind of space. And as one might expect from us, it is earth-plastered inside and out."

—Bill and Athena Steen

Opposite, top: The dimensions are 23 x 13 feet (7.01 x 3.96 meters) on the exterior. 200 square feet (18.58 square meters) on the interior. The glass wall faces the south. An adobe addition was added later to hide the water heater.

Opposite, bottom, left and center: The shower is contained within a curved adobe-cob wall that has a clay-mica-and-wheat-paste paint on the exterior and a lime-frescoed plaster on the interior. Apple juice jars embedded in clay function as inexpensive glass blocks.

Opposite, right: The bathroom walls are colored with a yellow-oxide casein wash. The ceiling is sheetrock covered with reed mats.

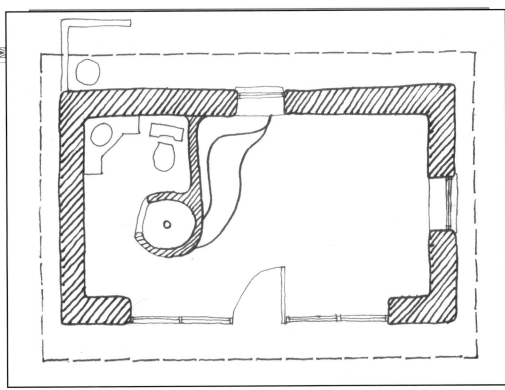

95

SHADING DEVICES

Clearly there are practical reasons for shading parts of a building—shade keeps the sun and light out of a given space, prevents overheating, and creates privacy. The same shading devices may also shield walls from the weather. Many can be made on-site from local materials. Shading devices can be as simple and uncomplicated as a tree or bush planted in the right location. Woven mats of reed, bamboo, or saguaro could be hung in front of a window, wall, or even better, they could be supported on a framework that arches outward to create a covered passageway. Lightweight structures that support vines, mats, screens, cloth, or branches could extend out from the edges of a building to create comfortable living and work areas beneath. By using deciduous plants and removable coverings, one can control when the sun and heat is let in or blocked out. Besides seasonal flexibility, shades, unlike porches, don't inhibit ventilation and can add a wonderful texture of light throughout and around a building.

In the western world, there is often an obsession with getting as much light as possible into the interior of a house. Even the phrase "casting a shadow" holds negative connotations. And although no one wants a dark house, perhaps something magical and mysterious is lost when everything becomes so evenly lit. The contrast created

Bill and Nancy's outdoor area shaded with wood trellises and vines.

between light and dark shadows adds dimension and character to a room. Patterns cast can be infinitely varied depending upon the nature of the screen, object, or plant used to create the shadow. One cannot help but remember the dark interiors of traditional Japanese buildings and the beauty of plant shadows cast upon delicate shoji screens—decoration so much more exquisite, simple, and alive than all the extraneous ornamentation that overfill modern-day homes.

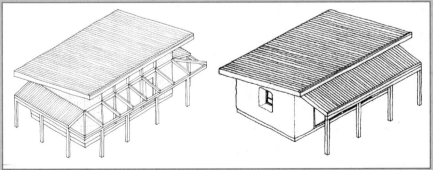

Sue Mullen's one-room shed building, in Gila, New Mexico, has protection on three sides that appropriately match the climatic need. On the east and south equator-facing side is a trellis for grapes that provides shade in the summer and yet allows the winter sun to pour in once the grapes lose their leaves. On the west side is a porch with metal roofing that provides rain and heavier shade protection.

ATHENA'S FIRST HOUSE

Glorieta Mesa, New Mexico

"As young college students, my first husband, Brian Reeves, and I built this simple 200-square-foot (18.58 square-meter) house in 1981. We were in desperate need of a house. My father had mentioned to us that we should build with straw. Having never heard of anyone doing it before, we just made it up as we went along. Not being carpenters, we decided on an easy-to-build shed roof with the higher end to the south for passive solar gain. Operating on very limited funds, we made double-paned plastic windows out of UV-treated plastic stapled to furring strip frames. On the interior of the windows were fifty-five gallon drums filled with water to provide thermal mass to store the winter day's heat and the summer night's coolness. The house stayed extremely comfortable year-round.

"We lived there for five years, three of them with small babies. Since it was such a small space, it had to be efficiently designed and everything had to do double duty. The built-in seat had a hinged plywood top that allowed for storage in the cavity. The raised bed provided storage below and later served as a tiny room for a crib. For winter showers, there was a small tub hidden under a trap door in the kitchen floor that drained to the outside. Our shower curtain was attached to a removable hula-hoop. We poured warm water from the stove into a suspended overhead bucket. By pulling on a rope attached to the bucket edge, we could regulate exactly how much water dumped out over us. In combination with a plunger, the sunken tub also worked as a low-tech washing machine."

—Athena Steen

Athena in front of bale walls.

Opposite: The dimensions are 12 x 23 feet (3.66 x 7.01 meters). Interior is 200 square feet (18.58 square meters).

Compact living with cooking, eating, sleeping, and storage all in one. Exterior dimensions 12 x 23 feet (3.66 x 7.01 meters), for 200 square feet (18.58 square meters) of interior space.

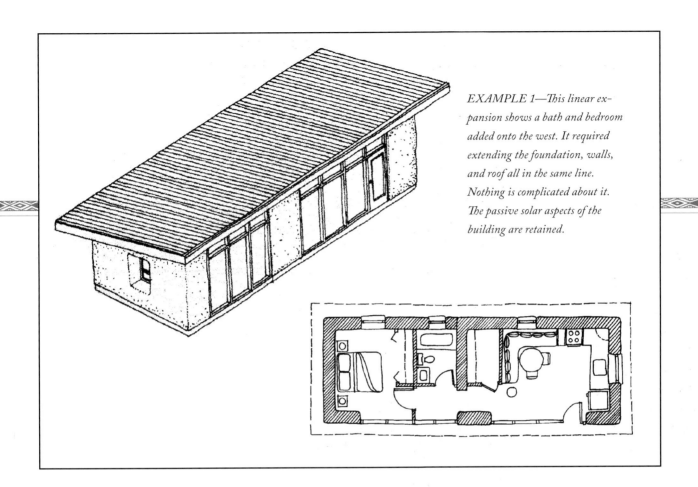

EXAMPLE 1—This linear expansion shows a bath and bedroom added onto the west. It required extending the foundation, walls, and roof all in the same line. Nothing is complicated about it. The passive solar aspects of the building are retained.

EXPANDING THE ONE-ROOM DESIGN

It is often easier and more manageable to first build a very small one-room structure, such as the structures shown in this chapter. Then when needed or as time dictates, it can be expanded in a variety of ways. Here are a couple of possible expansion schemes for adding on a bedroom and bathroom.

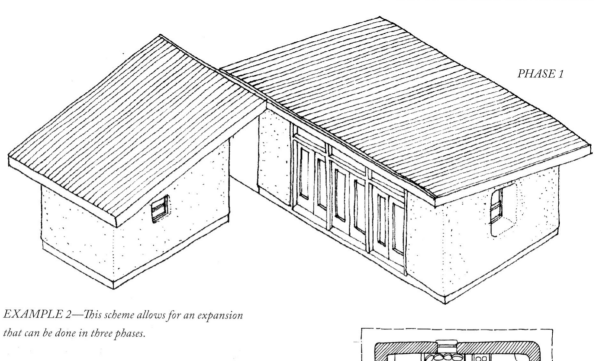

EXAMPLE 2—This scheme allows for an expansion that can be done in three phases.

PHASE 1: A bathroom could be added on with a connecting roof. A seasonal shade structure could be added on to shade the south glazing and form a patio area.

PHASE 2: An office/work area or storage/utility room plus bedroom could be added onto the west. Two separate patio spaces are developed, one more public off the main living space, the other off the bedroom.

PHASE 3: Eventually the patio area could be roofed and enclosed and used as a sunroom, or, with less glazing, could be converted into a large living area. The original house could then become a larger kitchen.

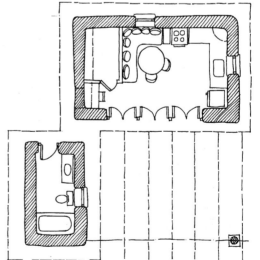

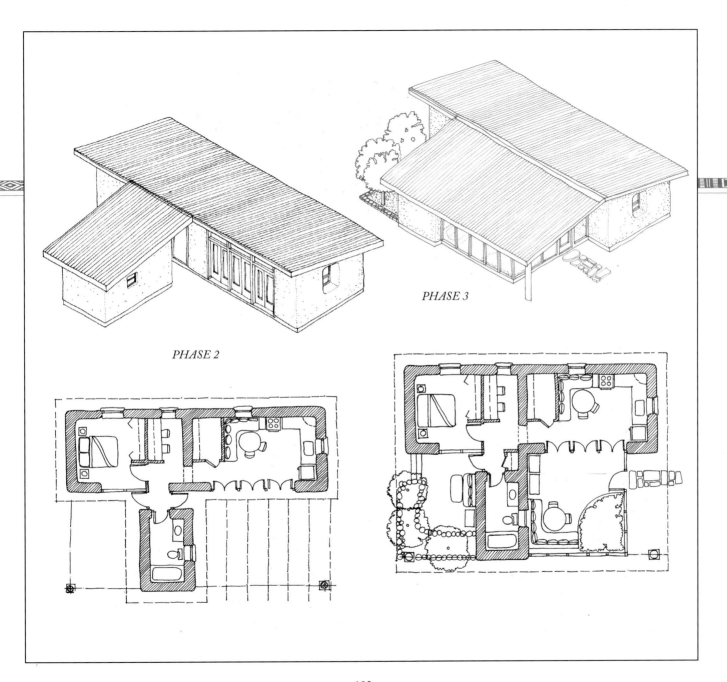

PHASE 2

PHASE 3

103

THE GABLE ROOF

For small buildings where there are high levels of rain or snow, the gable roof can be an excellent choice. It's relatively easy to build and enables one to achieve greater spans with smaller lumber sizes than are possible with a shed roof.

Trusses can be built on-site using nailed-on plywood; OSB or metal gussets at the connections; and press-on, spiked connector plates, bolts, or split-ring connectors through overlapping joints. Or someone who is handy with a torch might want to weld steel together to make trusses. Trusses, site-built or manufactured, offer many advantages that shouldn't be overlooked. They are engineered for material and structural efficiency.

A gable-roofed studio with wood shingles. Santa Sabino, California.

When scissor or parallel-chord trusses are used, the roof volume can be opened up to create usable space for an upper story or loft-mezzanine. They also make it possible to utilize generous amounts of insulation so that the roof complements the levels achieved by the bale walls.

Top: Gable made with rafters.
Middle, top: Flat-chord truss.
Middle, bottom: Parallel truss.
Bottom: Scissor truss.

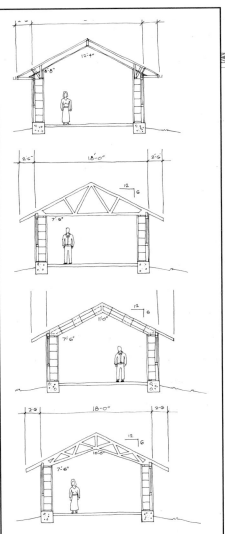

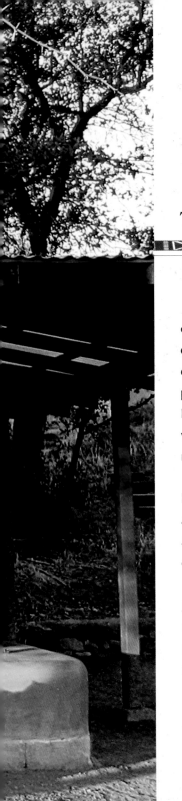

THE COTTAGE

Canelo, Arizona

The shelves and window molding are made from bamboo and straw-clay. The green bench is frescoed clay lime plaster.

"Thinking about this little building we call the Cottage, the first thing that comes to the mind is all the people who worked on it over the years. It was one of those projects that lingered on and on. We weren't in a hurry to finish it, nor did we have any particular vision of how it was supposed to look, so it became a place for friends, interns, and the like to try their hand at whatever inspired them. It is extremely small with an interior dimension of 8 x 9 feet (2.44 x 2.74 meters), which made it possible to focus on the kind of detail and finish work that would not have been possible had it been bigger.

"It was originally intended as a storage shed for tools and supplies, but halfway through its construction someone suggested that we add a loft due to the ample amount of space available beneath the gable roof. The suggestion took hold and far from being a tool shed, it became one of the most highly finished buildings on our property.

"After the basic structure of the building was constructed, the first person to get a hold of it was Frank Andresen, a German clay builder/plasterer. Not being a real public sort of person, he gravitated to its private space to work in peace and solitude. He completed demonstrations of various clay plaster samples, straw-clay wall panels and different clay ceiling techniques underneath the loft.

107

With an interior that is less than 100 square feet (9.29 square meters), the dimensions are 8-1/2 x 9 feet (2.59 x 2.74 meters). The loft is 8-1/2 x 6 feet (2.59 x 1.83 meters). The ceiling is bamboo with insulation. Above, the loft rafters were vaulted with reed mats, filled in with clay plaster, and then sponged back. The purple wall is lime and casein paint. The sidewalls are pure clay burnished to a polish.

"Many people have since worked on the cottage: our intern Ken meticulously cut and fit the glass in the gable ends; Emiliano Lopez worked on the shelves, window molding, and clay bench; John Woodin worked as a plastering partner; Steve Kemble worked as porch carpenter; and Satomi Lander worked with her Japanese characters. Many worked together to make it all come together in a unified whole. It's the way I like to think about the world as a whole: a bunch of random and different people working together to create something exquisite.

"There is so much clay in this building that the straw is almost incidental and secondary. Everything from the plaster to the floor, shelves, seating, loft ceiling, moldings, and straw-clay walls use clay as the base material. There is a small amount of lime plaster on the south wall since it is exposed to the weather and one interior wall for purple fresco color. The interior walls are highly polished clay that feel like a fine piece of pueblo pottery.

"It's been very enjoyable to figure out how small spaces can be used effectively. We've always been amazed at how comfortable and spacious the cottage feels. If one were to take full advantage of the porch to develop additional spaces, such as a south-facing sunroom for heating/sitting, a screen porch, storage, or a small kitchen, the cottage could be incredibly efficient and function as a small house. For now, it works beautifully for overnight visitors and interns."

—Bill Steen
The Canelo Project

Top, left: Two unburnished niches painted with the same clay as the walls.

Top, middle: A truth window showing the straw-clay wall sections around the door. The plaster is a high, straw-clay, one-coat plaster finished out.

Top, right: A truth window showing the bale wall and the rough-coat plaster beneath. The wall to the right was painted with linseed oil to bring out the contrast of the straw in the plaster.

109

ROOF SLOPE & PITCH

The slope of the roof, the size of the building, and the type of structure used for the roof will determine how much space is available within the volume of the roof.

Slope describes the incline of a roof as a ratio of the distance of a vertical rise to the distance of horizontal run. It is usually shown on drawings as a right-angle triangle where the inclination of the hypotenuse of the triangle matches that of the roof. The base of the triangle is always 12 units, which represents a horizontal run of 12 (from 12 inches per foot), and the altitude of the triangle represents the rise. Hence a slope of 4 in 12 (written as 4/12 or as a ratio 1:3) means that for every 12 units of horizontal run, there will be a 4-unit rise.

This relationship is useful in calculating the length of a rafter. For instance, on a building 24 feet (7.32 meters) wide that has a gable roof whose slope is 4/12, the horizontal run of the rafter will be 12 feet (3.66 meters) and its vertical rise will be 4 feet (1.22 meters). The line length of the rafter will be the square root of (16 + 144 = 160), or 12.65 feet (3.86 meters).

Pitch describes the incline of a roof as a ratio of the vertical rise to the span (twice the run). For instance, in the sketch, if the total rise is 4 feet (1.22 meters) and the total span is 24 feet (7.32 meters), then the pitch of the roof is 1/6 or a ratio of 1:6. The angle between the sloped portion and the horizontal in degrees would be about 18.5.

There is no best slope. Differing circumstances and needs will dictate varying approaches. For instance, in high-wind areas, it would be advantageous to decrease the slope of a roof to reduce the wind load, thereby reducing the structural requirements of the roof. Or, in areas that experience large amounts of rain or snow, it would be advantageous to use more steeply sloped roofs that quickly shed rain and snow, both to reduce the load that the roof structure will need to support and to minimize opportunities for leaks to occur. A roof that has a 30-degree pitch (or a 7/12

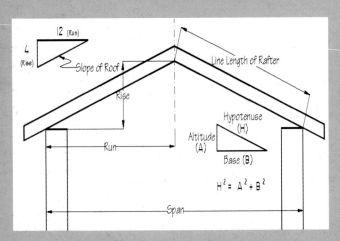

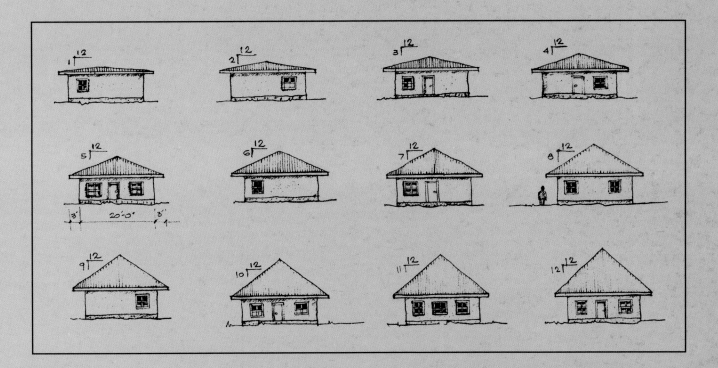

slope) is pretty close to being optimal from an engineering standpoint if the roof has to deal with both high winds and heavy rain or snow loads. The interior roof volume is typically adequate for useable, habitable space without the addition of unnecessarily high knee walls. The slope isn't so steep that you get tall, pointy ceilings that tend to be unusable volumes and which may be better suited for divine rather than mortal beings. Much steeper slopes are much more difficult to walk around on during construction and later when maintenance is required. Roofs with a slope of less than 2/12 or 1:6 are typically categorized as flat while those with more slope are regarded as pitched.

DIRK & MIRIAM'S STUDIO HOME

Guhreitzen, Germany

Miriam Joseph, Jiela Feline, and Dirk Scharmer.

"I built this studio as my small architectural office and bed place at the *empore* (the word *gallery* has the closest meaning in English). Very suddenly after the studio was completed, there appeared a woman, and twelve months later, our beautiful daughter Jiela Feline. Life is full of surprises. And so it happened that my small *atelier* became a dwelling for two and a half people. We enjoyed living there for eighteen months. We and all the people who visited us loved the rounded edges of the home and comfortable climate inside, which required only two arms of wood for heating in winter.

"My wife, a midwife, eventually wanted to leave the home because there weren't enough women to support her practice. We now live in a small town called Lueneburg, which is where my office is located. The new owners of our studio house are very pleased with it. They use it primarily for guests. They added central heating. We used a *badeofen,* which is a wood-fired, 100-litre water tank that heats very quickly. One of the things we liked most was being able to take a bath or shower in our open bathroom that overlooked the living room.

"The studio is 40 square meters or approximately 430 square feet. It started with a strip footing of concrete and crushed stone. Within the footing, we placed gravel followed by sand, polystyrene insulation, and strawbales covered with a mix of clay with straw. We then fastened a wooden floor of larch planks onto the foundation strips as a bearing for the bales and a place to attach wood post and beam framework.

Large three-string bales were placed on end. The walls were then plastered with clay and painted with lime casein.

The bales were stood on-end, which worked very well. We also hung strawbales from the rafters and plastered them above and below. This allowed us to avoid the use of another ceiling material. The plastered bales gave a very nice look. The strawbale walls were coated with clay plaster and lime-casein paint. We also applied a thin coat of lime plaster on the exterior walls. To ensure a good bond between the lime and substrate of clay plaster, we scored, or 'riffled,' the clay surface and applied a coating called *essigsaure tonderdeloesung*, which translates as aluminium potassium sulfate. Without this careful preparation, there would be a risk of the lime plaster delaminating, or falling off the wall."

—Dirk Scharmer

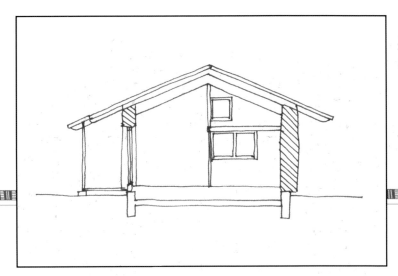

The building area is approximately 40 square meters (430.56 square feet). The loft runs over the back half of the house.

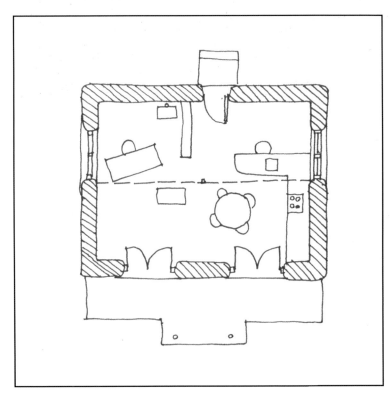

115

LOFTS & MEZZANINES

A loft or mezzanine can take advantage of extra ceiling space, thus increasing the usable space in smaller buildings. Depending on the ceiling height, a loft-mezzanine may be large enough to stand in, but if not, it can function as sleeping or storage space. In an open floor plan, by lowering the ceiling height, lofts can also help define smaller, more intimate areas beneath for cooking, eating, or bathing.

Lofts and mezzanines will have different requirements depending upon where they are built. For example, in many locations in the United States, there needs to be at least 7 feet (2.13 meters) of clear height above and below and can't exceed one-third of the area of the room or space in which a loft or mezzanine is located. However, for the purposes of this book, a loft or mezzanine in a small strawbale home might be built to dimensions that don't necessarily meet local requirements so long as code-required spaces are provided on the main floor. The loft or mezzanine could then be designated as storage space. If it eventually got used as a sleeping loft, then common sense should prevail: a railing should be installed so that people won't inadvertently fall off the loft level. A suitable means of ventilation and means of escape should also be provided in the event of a fire.

Lofts and mezzanines can be constructed in a number of ways. The floor can be attached to the perimeter beam at the top of the walls or built as a separate structure. An alternate approach would involve collar ties used to prevent the outward thrust of the rafters from spreading the walls apart. The creation of a loft or mezzanine can involve something as simple as placing some decking on top of the collar ties to make a floor.

A loft or mezzanine typically leaves two thirds or more of the floor area below open to the roof or to the next floor. If a main floor level has double-height ceilings, one might insert a loft or mezzanine over the utility areas where high ceilings wouldn't have much of an aesthetic effect.

A sleeping loft in an earth-floored, plastered strawbale home in Santa Fe, New Mexico.

A loft takes advantage of the entire volume of the gable roof in this off-the-grid strawbale bed and breakfast in Taos, New Mexico.

POEM'S HOUSE

Canelo, Arizona

"My sister, Poem, her husband, Arthur, and their two children, Dimitri and Sadie, are living in Evansville, Indiana. Their hearts, however, are in the Southwest. We decided to build a small house in Arizona that they could use at least during the summer and we could use as long-term guest quarters during other times of the year. Since money is always sparse, it had to be small and simple.

"We kept the house a simple rectangle so that the corrugated metal roof would be easy to construct. It is 30 feet (9.14 meters) long and 16 feet (3.66 meters) wide on the exterior—for a total of 350 square feet (32.53 square meters) on the interior. Two thirds of the interior space is an open kitchen, with an eating and sitting area. The other end has a king-size bed nook and a room for

bathing and clothes storage. Above is a loft where the kids sleep. On the south side, there will be a sunroom that will heat the house in the winter. A porch on the north side with small rooms at one end will be used for the sawdust toilet and battery storage since the house is off the grid. There is space nearby for a future bedroom/office.

"With the foundation in place, the walls and roof were completed during one of our weeklong strawbale workshops. Several excellent and hard-working carpenters in the group made the roof happen quickly.

"The walls were built with a method that is essentially a hybrid of load bearing and post and beam. The roof plate is pre-compressed using pairs of 3/8-inch (9.52-millimeter) threaded rod around the perimeter of the building. The

Workshop group putting gable scissor trusses and perlins in place.

Opposite, bottom left: Window and door bucks are braced onto the foundation, ready for bales.

Opposite, bottom middle: Three-string bales going up on edge in load-bearing fashion.

Opposite, bottom right: The walls have the first coat of straw-clay plaster. The roof is notched out for a sunroom addition.

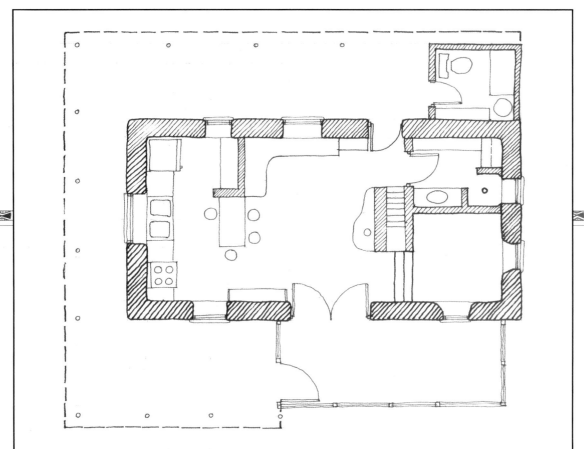

The exterior dimensions are 30 x 16 feet (9.14 x 4.88 meters). The interior is 350 square feet (32.53 square meters). A sleeping loft is over the bed nook and bathing area. The steps up to it are behind an adobe wall and cob fireplace.

plate is then compressed until it comes into contact with the door and window frames that run from foundation to roof plate. Exterior bamboo pins (two pairs per bale), or ribs as some call them, are also cut to the same height as the door/window frames so the roof plate, once it is compressed comes into contact with them as well. Tied tightly against the bales, they act like mini posts. Further settling of the walls is avoided, leaving a rock-solid wall in place that is immediately ready for earth plaster. One day we left our old 1952 International truck with a dysfunctional parking brake running in neutral parked on a slope some thirty feet away. Overpowering the parking break, the truck rolled into the side of the building before any

120

plaster had been applied. The walls didn't budge an inch.

"Other features that have become important to us over the years were or will be incorporated into the house. The foundation was oversized enough to allow the earth plasters to rest on it without coming into contact with the ground. All exposed windows that aren't under porches have sills. The roof and floor are insulated with generous amounts of insulation—in this case, cellulose in the ceiling and pumice beneath the earth floor.

"Once finished and sculpted out, we hope the house will demonstrate not only sound building techniques but will also serve as a reminder that perhaps we don't need more space; we just need to make what space we do have more efficient, comfortable, and beautiful."

—Athena Steen
The Canelo Project
www.caneloproject.com

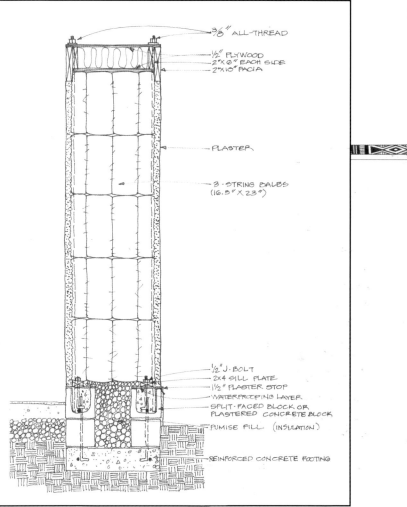

The wall section of an all-thread compression system.

ONE-AND-A-HALF-STORY BUILDINGS

The term one-and-a-half story typically refers to a house where the second floor or story is contained within the volume of the roof. Sometimes a short knee or pony wall is used on top of the lower walls to gain additional height and room.

By taking advantage of the space within the roof volume by using rafters or parallel-chord trusses, the space can perform the added function of housing people rather than a jungle of web members as is the case when using triangular trusses. There are many good reasons why it makes sense to utilize upper-level living space instead of spreading out horizontally. There is the reduced impact on a site: a smaller foundation (less concrete, less work, and less insulation material); possibly half the amount of roof area; and lower operating costs. It makes even more sense in cold climates. At night, the upper levels will have accumulated the heat from the day and will remain cozy for sleeping.

On the other hand, the use of the volume within the roof may increase the structural requirements. The structure needed to support habitable space is greater than that required for uninhabited attic space. Where wind and seismic concerns are an issue, additional lateral strength may be necessary. It should also be understood that the space where the angle of the roof intersects with the floor area may have little value except for storage. There are also access requirements; and, in a small house, stairs and the area needed to access them can take up a lot of space. It may be that an alcove, a bump-out or extension on the length of the building can give the desired result with less complications, cost, and with greater ease.

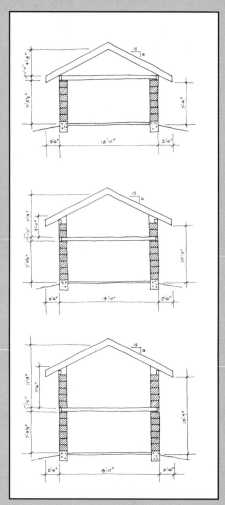

Top: Simple gable with no additional wall height.
Middle: One-and-a-half story with a two-bale knee wall.
Bottom: Mezzanine with one-and-a-half story, five bales.

DORMERS

Dormers can significantly increase headroom, add light, and increase ventilation. They can be particularly useful in expanding the area in a loft or upper story. For the most part, the shed dormer is the easiest to build and provides the greatest increase in useful area. A short knee or pony wall could further increase the volume of the space.

Shed dormer. Hidden Villa (near Los Altos), California.

PROTECTING THE GABLE END WALLS

One of the weakest aspects of a gable roof is the lack of overhangs on the gable ends, which leave those walls less protected. The lower portion of the gable end is easily protected by a wraparound continuation of the eaves, overhangs, or porch, but the upper part of the gable end wall can be a challenge to protect. The simplest solution is to make most of the wall out of materials that are immune to rain wetting. Windows would fit this criteria as would a pressure-equalized ventilated-rainscreen assembly. Or the eaves of the gable end could be extended enough to create a sheltered walkout for the upper story.

A kitchen alcove extension adds extra usable space and protects gable-end walls. Dave Clark's house in Moab, Utah.

SMALL HOUSES

A decorated niche and window molding of Mexican tiles under the porch of Carol Robert's house. Tucson, Arizona.

Genuinely small houses are difficult to find in today's world. We live in an age of "mansionization" and "starter castles" where the house has become a fortress to encase the family and protect it from the sterile and hostile environment that surrounds it. The belief that bigger is better continues to drive the size, cost, and material and energy use steadily upwards. In 1952, houses in the United States averaged 290 square feet (26.95 square meters) per family member. By 1997, that number had increased to 800 square feet (74.35 square meters) per member. Larger houses with their complex geometry, additional features, and tall ceilings use proportionately more materials. And even though modern houses are better insulated and more energy efficient, they normally consume considerably more energy than small, inefficient houses.

The houses in this section range from 300 square feet (27.88 square meters) to just over 1,200 feet (11.52 square meters). They are small and uncomplicated with high doses of natural materials and owner-built involvement. Their floor plans are rectangular in shape (except for one), which helps keep costs and required skill levels low. Not ridden with fancy architectural details, they quietly reflect the soul and character of their owners and builders. They all provide adequate spaces for living, cooking, sleeping, and bathing, yet don't necessarily have the "correct" number of bedrooms, bathrooms, and square feet demanded by commercial resale values.

In the words of Canadian designer and builder John Salmen:

> The basic issue is that we construct too much. We build buildings to house materials and stuff . . . and then construct landfills (underground buildings for all practical purposes) to house the materials and stuff removed from buildings to make room for more materials and stuff. When I ask a client to spend twice as much to build half the space, they view this as a negative. In other words their unspoken goal is as much space for as little upfront cost as possible. There is little appreciation of the long-term service, maintenance and ultimate environmental costs of the large, cheap spaces because these are fairly abstract concepts to deal with when the exigencies appear to be affordable large spaces.

Compact kitchen beneath a small sleeping loft. Patagonia, Arizona.

PHIL & SHERRI'S GUESTHOUSE

Patagonia, Arizona

"The quaintness of our guesthouse belies its origins as a tomato-packing shed. Its quirky evolution owes a great deal to the flexibility of strawbale construction and our contractor, Ted Piper. We work in the organic produce industry and had a tomato-packing shed on the U.S.-Mexico border. It was a simple structure with a tin roof attached to steel arches. The tin kept disappearing panel by panel at night, however, so we decided to dismantle the building and store it on our land. It wound up in a pile in a lovely meadow where it was an eyesore until we decided it could be put to better use as a kayak shed. At the time we were living in an airstream trailer while we designed our house. Our ocean kayaks were baking in the harsh Arizona sunlight, and we thought the tomato shed would be perfect to house them in along with construction materials when we began to build.

"We contacted a local contractor who referred us to Ted. Ted did not seem to mind launching a project without a blueprint, materials list, or even a budget. We had taken a course in strawbale construction in preparation for building our house and Ted also had experience with strawbale so we naturally decided the shed would be a good beginning project. The tomato shed determined the shape of the kayak shed. We framed our footings with river stones gathered from the property and poured the cement. Then we began to lay the bales. But as the structure went up, we realized that it was pretty large and much too interesting to remain a simple shed.

"We weren't sure what the building would

127

become, but we decided to put in some elements that would create options for the future. We integrated some small windows and put in wiring for electricity. As more walls went up, the structure began to feel more like a dwelling, and we began to envision a possible guesthouse. Luckily we had decided on a poured adobe floor, so it wasn't too difficult to trench in plumbing for a bathroom and kitchen sink. The challenge was how to create a bathroom, kitchen, bedroom, and living room out of 360 square feet (33.46 square meters). After endless sketches on napkins, the solutions began to surface. The shed was fairly tall, arching up to 15 feet (4.57 meters), so we had vertical space to create a loft above the kitchen and bathroom to be used as sleeping area. The bathroom would feature a Mexican-style open shower that shared a compact room with a sink and composting toilet. The kitchen would have a wraparound counter, a tiny stove, and a Swedish Vestfrost refrigerator, which is taller and narrower than the standard American fridge. This left a

fairly generous area for a small table, couch, armoire, and woodstove.

"The two big challenges were to create a stairway to the loft that did not eat up the living space and that could be navigated easily in the dark. The second challenge was to bring daylight into a structure that had few windows. Building a marine-type ladder with a good handrail solved the stairway problem. It is easily navigable even in the sleepiest state. Light was brought in at the ends of the guesthouse. The roof arches in the center, so we simply finished the strawbales on the side at the same level as the front and back walls and used glass to complete the triangular space at either end of the building.

"We built the initial structure for about $4,000 in materials. The windows were salvaged from western movie sets. The doors were salvaged from a hotel in Tucson. A skylight into the bathroom from the loft is a large pane of glass from the VA Hospital. The plaster on the inside and outside of the building was made from

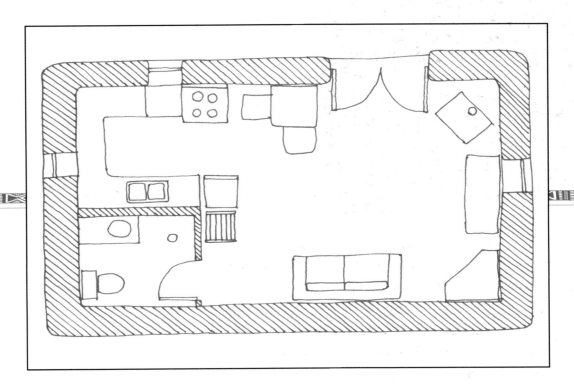

The house has a 288-square-foot (26.76-square-meter) interior. Dimensions are 12 x 24 feet (3.66 x 7.32 meters).

clay from the property, sand, carpenter's glue, and horse manure. The floor is poured adobe, coated with linseed oil and turpentine. The only major new material purchases included tongue-and-groove pine for the ceiling and Mexican tile for the kitchen and bathroom.

"The house is very comfortable in the summer with an evaporative cooler and stays toasty in the winter with a small fire in the woodstove. We mastered some invaluable skills while building, not the least of which was to keep our strategic planning and architectural renderings twenty-four hours ahead of the construction crew. Besides being very functional, the house is lovely to look at and fits beautifully into our canyon environment. Our casita, as we called it, would become our home for two years. It was very wonderful to live in such an efficient and charming space. You can imagine my surprise when one morning my wife began to discuss her ideas for our 'house' when I thought we were already living in it."

—Phil Ostrom
New Harvest Organics
www.newharvestorganics.com

ALCOVES

Alcoves can be some of the most comfortable, fun, and interesting spaces. They have a separateness and identity all their own even though they are connected to and part of a larger room. Partial walls, curtains, screens, plants, and even a furniture arrangement can "enclose" and define a nook-like space. A simple change in color, texture, or floor and ceiling height might even be enough. Alcoves usually project out beyond the perimeter of the room, but they may also be developed within the existing space, as long as they function as quiet and intimate places where one or a few people can retreat to sleep, sit and relax, eat, or converse without completely leaving the activities of the main and more public room.

Smaller houses with open floor plans can potentially lose the defined spaces that can be necessary for specific activities. Most modern houses take care of this by adding additional rooms yet alcoves can often meet those same needs without the complexity of construction and additional space. Bedrooms, offices, and dining rooms can be eliminated, thus reducing square footage and cost. Additionally, small rooms can often feel cramped and uncomfortable while alcoves are warm, cozy, and inviting.

A child's bed alcove in the Husted's home. Bayfield, Colorado.

130

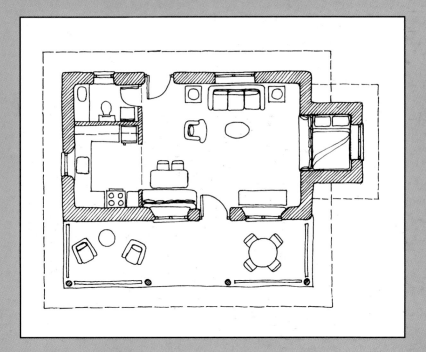

Modified floor plan of Phil and Sherri's home shows a bed alcove off the main room. It also has a back door with a north porch addition.

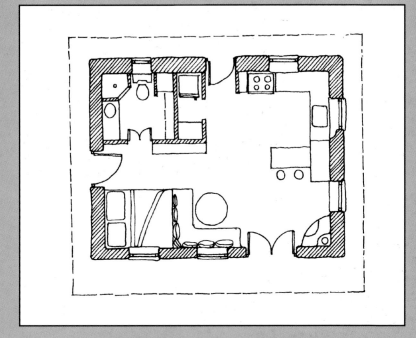

This conceptual floor plan is for a 20 x 16-foot (6.10 x 4.88-meter) interior with two-string bales used for the walls. The interior is 320 square feet (29.74 square meters). The exterior is 24 x 20 feet (7.32 x 6.10 meters). The raised bed in the lower left corner creates an alcove-like space with storage below. The bed also functions as a back for the seating area.

STERLING & HEIDI'S HOUSE

Near Davis, California

The small square windows allow light in from the west without radiating too much heat. The cement stucco was stained with ferrous sulfate.

Opposite: The interior with sleeping loft above the pantry and bath. The walls are finished with earth plasters. The floor is Mexican saltillo tile.

"Though we had the opportunity to build on bare land, we were completely inexperienced and unprepared, both financially and conceptually to take on the task of building a full-blown 'dream house.' Our goal was just to get something up that we could live in. We were even so naive as to imagine that we might build our 'real' house later on a different site. In that event, however, we didn't want our first building to become obsolete, so we conceived of it as an agricultural building, a greenhouse, or an office.

"We were always attracted to alternative buildings and environmentally sound structures in particular. Our primary influence at the time came from our experiences in Colorado building earthships. Strawbale struck us as an alternative building material that was, however, more suitable to conditions in northern California. Thus we contacted Bob Theis of Dan Smith and Associates, and he promptly drew up for us what was effectively a strawbale earthship. The plan was simple, compact, and affordable. And yet it allowed for all the provisions of a basic residence. We have been extremely happy with this space. It has functioned great as a passive solar building, requiring only minimal backup heating, and it has remained cool and comfortable in the summer.

"Shortly after starting this project, however, it became clear to us that there would be no other 'real' house. This was it. With the birth of our daughter, we also realized that we would grow out of this space before too long, so even before we finished we were thinking of how to

add on. We have since added on an entry/living room and soon plan to add a bedroom wing. Yet the original building will remain the core of the house with the kitchen and dining area being the central gathering and activity hub.

"Throughout this ongoing project we have done everything ourselves and have done it all out of pocket. It is slower this way, but it has saved us a lot of money and enabled us to spend more on finishing details than we might have otherwise. The construction took us two and a half years. A bedroom wing, however, will require us to take out a loan or else it will never happen. Since we all sleep together in the loft, I hope to get that done before my daughter becomes a teenager."

—Sterling Keene

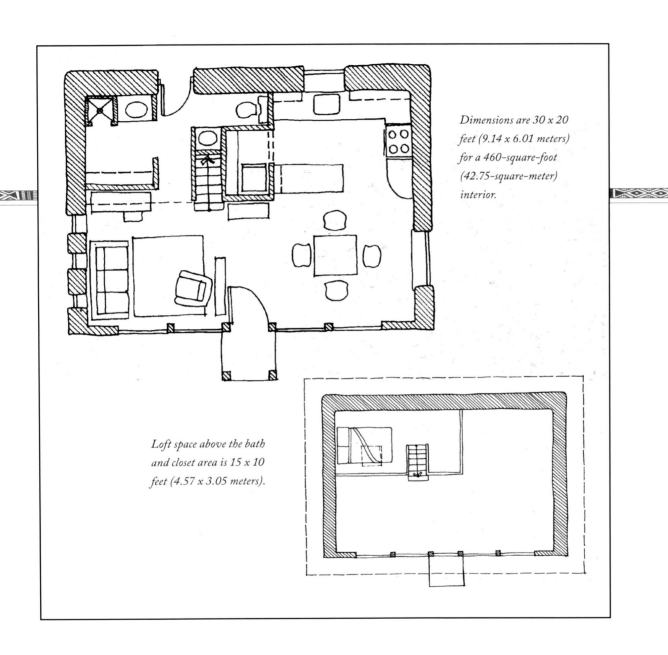

Dimensions are 30 x 20 feet (9.14 x 6.01 meters) for a 460-square-foot (42.75-square-meter) interior.

Loft space above the bath and closet area is 15 x 10 feet (4.57 x 3.05 meters).

ERIC & LAURIE'S HOME

Bayfield, Colorado

"I was skeptical of strawbale when Laurie and I first saw it in a video in the early 1990s. How could such a simple idea be workable—stack some bales and build a roof on top? But while researching, I came across McClintocks' *Alternative Housebuilding* in the Fresno Public Library. While it doesn't mention strawbale, it made me start questioning conventional framing. A weekend visit to Tucson for a workshop was the first time we actually touched and went inside a strawbale structure. After taking a permaculture design course, we could see the benefits of strawbale for our chosen topography and climate.

"In the fall of 1992, we traveled the Four Corners area looking for land and bought thirty-five acres about twenty miles east of Durango, Colorado, at about 7,600 feet (2,316.48 meters) in elevation in a ponderosa pine and gambel oak forest that can get 20 inches (508 millimeters) of precipitation a year (but hasn't seen that for several years). We have four distinct seasons with summer high temperatures in the 90s and winter days almost always dropping to just above freezing. Spring and fall tend to be cool and windier with a good portion of our 300 sunny days coming in the shoulder seasons. The temperature swings are often 30 to 40 degrees Fahrenheit (-1.11 to 4.44 degrees Celsius) on a daily basis. Our high-mass earthen and flagstone floor combined with the straw insulation keeps the indoor temperature swings to just a few degrees year round.

"We started out wanting to build in the round or octagonally, but when I began scale drawings I settled on a one-story rectangular shed with room all the way around to add on. Going small (16 x 32 feet = 512 square feet or 47.58 meters inside) to start with kept initial costs down. We paid cash for our land, and, two years later, in mid-September, we moved into a trailer on the land with $12,000

Eric harvesting local timber with his horses.

Opposite: Added on to the main straw-bale structure is this wood slated entry-way with cordwood foundation.

137

saved up and Laurie seven months pregnant. I boldly predicted that Kyla would be born in the new house.

"Our county codes required a post and beam system so we dug and poured a perimeter foundation with bump-ins for the posts to rest on and a slab for the bales to the exterior. We bolted together bents of round logs we had cut and peeled the winter before.

"Kyla was born in the 16-foot (4.88-meter) trailer on October 30, 1994. The roof and soffit were completed during November. Ninety percent of the wood was either cut and milled on-site or salvaged. On December 4, with the help of new friends and neighbors, we raised the walls. Over thirty showed up on Saturday morning and by Sunday evening we had walls and the smaller floating windows installed. We cut bales to fit around the larger openings that had foundation-to-rafter framing. We added a woodstove, windows, and tarps for doors. We moved in before Christmas.

"Now, almost ten years later, we have added a sleeping loft, mudroom, and cold storage/mechanical room bermed into the north for 818 square feet (76.00 square meters) of interior space. We also added a west-side sleeping deck that affords dawn views of the LaPlatas from April through October for another 325 square feet (30.20 square meters) of outside covered space. We all slept in the loft until Kyla was seven. Laurie and I now sleep there when the early winter storms drive us in from the west deck. We have plans for a bathroom and bedroom addition on the north and a sunroom to the south as Kyla grows and needs a bigger space than afforded by the built-in daybed she now calls her room. So far we have about $40,000 invested in the house, including a photovoltaic system and water collection system with about 9,000 (34,069 liters) gallons of storage. The drought of the last six years relented a bit this past winter and things have greened up and allowed us to do some more landscaping."

—Eric Husted

A flagstone walkway runs through the middle of the earth floor sealed with linseed oil.

PATRICIA'S CASITA

Big Bend, Texas

A seat made from old wood and cob.

Opposite: Patricia Kearn sitting on a cob bench in front of her house.

"My journey to a small place began with a simple desire for financial independence. Several years ago, having taken an early retirement from my employer, I needed to find a way to live on less than half my previous income. I had to reduce fixed expenses, especially my mortgage payment. The crazy idea that I could find some cheap land and build a house with my own two hands began to work its way into my head.

"How crazy was that idea? I was a forty-some-year-old attorney whose only experience with a hammer was hanging diplomas. I didn't even have a high school shop class to draw on for experience. I ran through these and other pertinent obstacles every day, trying to get the goofy idea that I could build my own home out of my head. When the chance to attend a workshop on strawbale building came along I jumped at it, thinking I could finally prove to myself that I couldn't do it. But that workshop, as well as the work I did at several succeeding work sites, made it clear to me that my dream could be realized.

"I began planning my home's design as I sought land and prepared to move to a small desert community in the Big Bend area of southwestern Texas, far from any big cities. As I developed the design, I realized the house would have to be very small if I wanted to complete it myself. I originally considered this to be a limitation, but one that I was willing to accept. I imagined that my standard of living in terms of creature comforts would decline, but I accepted this as a small price to pay to free myself from the burden of a mortgage.

141

"I got some excellent advice, however, at one of the subsequent workshops I attended. I was challenged to record the amount of time I spent in every area of my home for a week. I was living in a small 1,100-square-foot (102.23-square-meter) home when I conducted this experiment. I was amazed to find that there were two rooms in my home where I rarely set foot. I realized with a shock that the primary purpose of those two rooms was to store furniture that I had only bought so those rooms wouldn't be empty. This was a happy realization, since all I had to do to cut my space needs in half was sell furniture!

"I sold every piece of furniture I owned at multiple garage sales. After two months of shedding stuff accumulated over twenty years, I packed what was left into a 10 x 6-foot (3.05 x 1.83-meter) U-Haul trailer, hitched it to the back of my truck, and headed for Texas. I had never felt so free in my life. It was the first sign that living in a small space wasn't going to be the dip in my standard of living that I had imagined.

"I spent the first three months in Texas camping out of my Suburban in a national park while looking for land. This was a good start to my new commitment to minimalism. In January 1998, I moved onto a piece of unspoiled desert land halfway between the communities of Lajitas and Terlingua, Texas. I erected a 16 x 16–foot (4.88 x 4.88-meter) army tent, built a composting toilet and solar oven, set up a solar shower and camp stove, and hooked up some solar panels. I was living in the lap of luxury!

"It took about two months to get my casita's foundation built and the strawbale walls up, just in time to have a spot to get out of the severe winds that whipped across my land in February and March. I had no roof, no windows, no doors, and no floor, but it was a wonderfully comfortable spot to sit and read or play my guitar while the winds howled outside. I could never before have appreciated such a humble shelter. It seemed like heaven to me.

"I spent six months finishing the exterior, roof, doors, and windows, and then moved into the house while I finished the interior. I had designed a space that included a bedroom, small computer nook, and larger sitting room. The design was a circular space trisected into three areas. Between the three areas, instead of building walls, I built shelves that pass through so they can be utilized from either side. This gave me a great deal of storage in a small space.

The bed is a futon on a plywood board that flips up to reveal storage. I also designed a built-in sofa in the sitting area with storage underneath. I learned a lot about effective use of small spaces for storage by visiting numerous trailer sales lots to study trailer design. All of my interior furniture is built-in, using cob and scrap wood.

"I decided not to have the kitchen and bathroom in the main house, but rather to leave them for a second project. I haven't regretted this decision. I continue to be happy cooking on a camp stove or in a solar oven and using a camp shower and composting toilet. The climate here is quite mild, so this might not be feasible in a more northern location. I learned to live with so little during my journey here that every addition now seems like an invaluable luxury.

"My home is circular, 20 feet (6.10 meters) in diameter, with a 2-foot (609.60-millimeter) diameter post made of cob in the center. This gives me a little over 250 round feet (23.23 round meters) of floor space. I lived here for a year quite comfortably on my own, but this year I acquired a partner. We have managed to both fit comfortably into the same space. (Don't try this with someone you don't like a lot!)

"One of the benefits of my decision to build small became apparent as I networked with other self-builders. I was able to complete my home in the same amount of time that people needed to build larger structures, but I used much less labor. This allowed me to like the home and keep liking it as I worked. I never felt overwhelmed by the process. My little casita and I have remained fast friends, and I have nothing but good memories and good energy invested in my home.

"I enjoy what I have now far more than four times the stuff I used to have. My home and possessions serve and shelter me, and are never a burden that require more than I am willing to give (such as a thirty-year mortgage). I am well on my way to becoming sustainable on this land, and a small home is part of what allowed me to see my way there. Now, whenever I am inside large enclosed spaces, I feel lost, disassociated, and adrift. I wouldn't trade my casita or my experience of creating it for a mansion any day. Responding to the site and our needs, and building the house day by day have been the most satisfying and meaningful experiences of our lives."

—Patricia Kearn
www.twistedroad.com

VARIATIONS ON LARGER CIRCULAR BUILDINGS

Even though the area of each of these circular buildings is larger than the small dwellings we have included here, we discuss them because they are similar in shape to Patricia Kearns' house. Interest in round buildings has been significant and there are many features to consider. A circular enclosure utilizes the least amount of wall surface to enclose a specific interior space.

There are some technical issues that should be recognized if you are considering a round building. Laying out the foundation is rather easy, but forming a round foundation wall and putting wood nailers on it utilizes wood that is different from the linear type you buy at the lumberyard. That goes also for the roof plate on the bales, although you might be able to use a set of straight, short pieces to approximate the round shape. Radial rafters can be supported at a central point or a conical roof can be built where the rafters meet at the apex without the need of a central support. For that matter, unless there is an upper story, radial rafters aren't needed or required. Roof sheathing and the roofing material will need to be cut into pie-shaped pieces. Gutters are usually fabricated in straight pieces.

You need to give some thought to the layout of the interior spaces. The variations illustrated here show the need for curved cabinetry in kitchen and bathroom spaces. Curved interior walls may need to be built of some kind of masonry—for example, adobe, cob, or straw-clay blocks. They can receive the same earthen

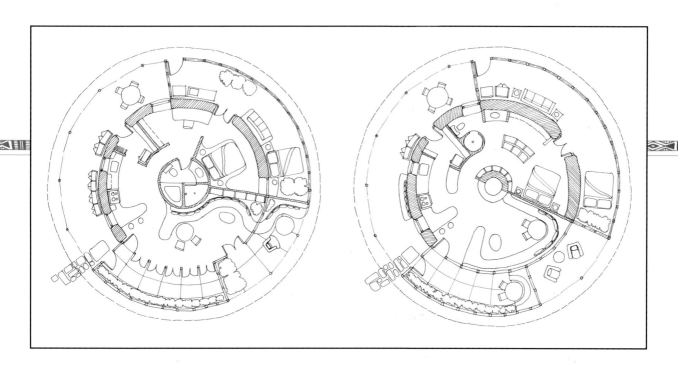

plaster as the exterior walls. Circular walls can be made of wood studs and gypsum board, but they require a good amount of focused effort.

Given the time, effort, and complexity associated with shaping materials into a round form, the cost of building normally reflects that complexity. Even though circular walls enclose the space most efficiently, they can seldom be built in a material-efficient and cost-efficient manner.

With a 13.8-foot (4.21-meter) radius, for an approximately 600-square-foot (55.76-square-meter) interior. Greenhouse off the south. Screen porch off the north. Bathroom walls in center supply support for the roof.

BUILT-IN FURNITURE

Built-in furniture is an efficient way to conserve space and an alternative to buying expensive manufactured furniture. It can be custom shaped to fit an odd space and used to "fill in" and soften the corners of a room, dramatically changing its character.

Although furniture is typically made from wood, it is also possible to make shelves, beds, seating, counters, and tables from clay. Beds and seats can be built using blocks (adobes or straw clay) or a cob-like mix that is formed or molded to outline the desired shape. Stones, bricks, or masonry block can be used for the bottom course to provide extra resistance to abrasion from shoes and water. The hollow center can be filled and compacted with stone, dirt, or sand. Using dense materials also provides good thermal mass. If storage is needed, the interior of the bed or seat can be left hollow and a top can be made from wood that is hinged or from slides.

Shelves, counters, and tables can be made in several ways. The uprights can be built either using clay blocks,

An entertainment center in Roxanne Swentzell's studio made from clay, straw, and bamboo. Santa Clara, New Mexico.

which is the fastest method, or a frame can be made from bamboo or branches that are wrapped with a mix of clay and straw. It is also possible but slower to use a cob-like mix by itself without the frame.

The top of the shelf, counter, or table can be formed in three basic ways:

1. The least complicated is to lay horizontal pieces of bamboo or branches between the uprights and cover them with a mix of clay and straw.
2. Another is to mold a wet mix of clay and straw in the shape of an arch over a form that can be removed when the mix is dry.
3. Or, with a little bit of knowledge about masonry techniques, small clay blocks can be laid over arched formwork that is removed as soon as the blocks are in place. Moist sand supported by a piece of plywood can work as a simple formwork.

Depending upon the type of wear to which shelves, counters, or tables will be subjected, different surface treatments are possible. For light wear, several coats of linseed oil will usually suffice although they will darken the color. If the surface is expected to withstand heavier wear, lime plaster, wire-reinforced cement plaster or concrete can be used as the top. Colored and polished, plaster or concrete can provide beautiful contrast and color.

A cob bench follows the curve of the walls. Michael Smith's house in Oregon.

Straw-clay and carrizo shelves in the office of Save the Children in Obregon, Sonora, Mexico.

CAROLYN'S HOUSE

Tucson, Arizona

Carolyn Roberts

Opposite: Carolyn's house sits in the middle of the Sonoran Desert.

"I love to be out in nature, contemplating the meaning of life. I find the pressure to earn and spend money quite annoying. Nature gives us so many free gifts that help us survive that I don't see why I have to pay for everything. I have felt confounded as to why our society continues to multiply the stress and complexity of life rather than looking for simple solutions. Mankind has lived on this planet for thousands of years without credit cards and mortgages, so I thought that by studying older cultures I could find a way to step back into their simpler lifestyle. To me it seemed a more joyful, friendlier way of life. Natural building was my way of taking a step back and a step forward.

"I had never thought about building a house until I learned about natural building. It seemed that by using forgiving materials from the earth and having work parties, I could do much of the work myself with the help of unskilled laborers. However, I always imagined that I would have a husband heading up the project. I didn't have any thought of doing this myself until I was suddenly divorced and financially strained. By that time, I had been studying natural building for eight years and felt adverse to every house that did not consider the angles of the sun in its design. Since I had to move, I decided

149

Above the bedroom and bath is a loft for extra sleeping.

to make it a positive move into a natural home that encompassed what I had been studying. My desire was so strong at that point that I didn't really understand the difficulty of what I was taking on. Necessity prodded me into doing something I wouldn't have imagined possible.

"I first designed a house that was 1,500 square feet (139.35 square meters) for my two teenagers and me. To me, at the time, that was small and simple. When I did a workshop with the Steens, however, they urged me to reduce the size of my house in order to reduce both the cost and construction workload. I was reluctant, but then Athena reminded me that my two boys would only be home for about five more years so it wouldn't make sense to burden myself with

a thirty-year mortgage on a larger house. I really liked the floor plan developed by Wayne, Bill, and Athena. It was a large open room with a loft and surrounding porch. The loft seemed like a good solution to provide living quarters for my boys, and the sunroom would provide passive solar heating and natural lighting. I saw that a smaller house was something that could still fulfill our needs, be attractive, and be affordable.

"The house has been a long story filled with adventure, romance, and a happy ending that is best told in my book, *A House of Straw*. I was fed up with life after many dead ends. I was determined to find a way to live independently, close to nature, and with dignity. I was so resolute and had such a short time

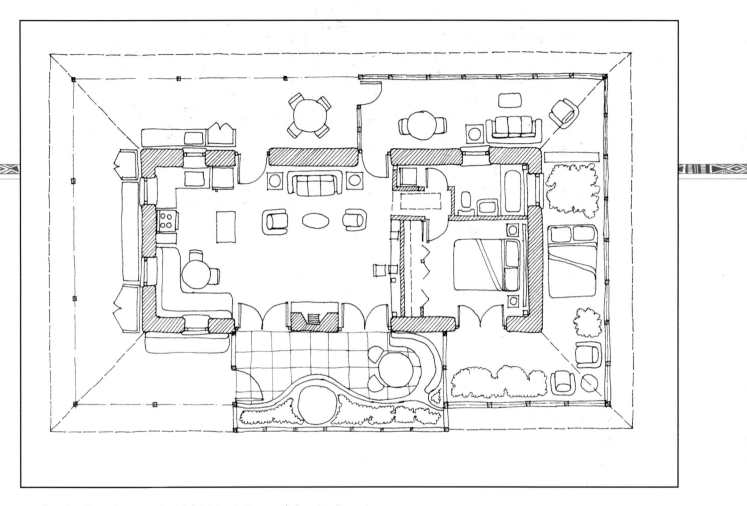

Exterior dimensions are 42 x 18 (12.80 x 5.49 meters). Interior dimensions are 756 square feet (70.23 square meters). Storage loft is 288 square feet (26.76 square meters). Sunroom is 220 square feet (20.43 square meters). Screened porch is 427 square feet (39.67 square meters). Other porch area is 569 square feet (52.86 square meters).

Scissor trusses were used to create an open ceiling, which allowed the roof cavity to be turned into a loft.

frame in which to build that I charged into this construction without really understanding what I was doing. I went through many trials for this reason, but I made it through them all mostly as a result of sheer resolve, a good consultant, many people who came to help, and divine intervention—not necessarily in that order.

"Some of the most important things I learned were: get in physical shape before you begin, be willing to let go of everything during the building process, do lots of good deeds before you begin so you will have friends and favors coming your way, find a good consultant and have a financial plan B because it will cost more than you think. Most importantly, enjoy the process!

"What distinguishes this house for me and gives it a comfortable and relaxed quality is the presence of so many natural textures: strawbale walls, earthen plasters and floors, reed ceilings, and colorful Mexican tile. Since I had only small areas to finish, I could afford to use quality materials and pay attention to the details. By doing so much of the labor myself, this house became an experience rather than a purchase— a home rather than an investment. It's simple, but it's beautiful.

"The sunroom is one of my favorite features with its large windows overlooking the desert and my cockatiel aviary. It's also great for growing plants and sprouting seeds in the winter. During the hot summer, I close the French doors

152

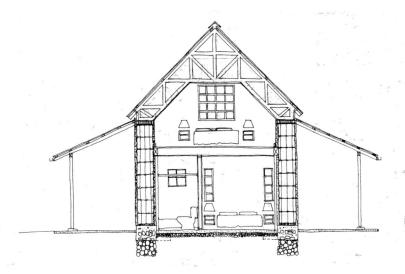

to keep the heat out of the house but still allow natural light into the main room. On cold winter nights, I can likewise shut off the sunroom to insulate the house. During the winter days, I open the doors and allow the passive solar heat into the main room.

"If I were to do the project today, I would have more knowledge, more time, more money, and more help. The biggest pressure of building was the time constraint; I had to keep chugging ahead even when I was exhausted. Building a house is more work than anyone can imagine. I have heard that generally a person's biggest regret at the end of their house construction is that they built too large; I don't have that regret. There's really not much I'd do differently.

"I didn't have a lot of time to do much scrounging. I work full time and spent every evening and weekend building since I was under such time pressure. My only time to gather materials was during my lunch hours. So I found a couple of recycle stores near my office and visited them often. All my windows and doors are recycled. They saved me a lot of money

"The house cost about $50,000, not including land, or about $40 per square foot. It was really by doing so much of the labor myself that I saved the most money. If I hadn't had to pass twenty-four building inspections, I think I could have built for much less. I had about $25,000 to my name, so I put a minimum down on the land and made payments to the seller until the house was complete. I saved as much money as I could for house construction. I didn't want the requirements and time limits of a construction loan; a bank wouldn't have let me do much of the work myself. My parents helped, I sold my car, and I got a signature loan from my credit union to complete the house. Then when the house was completed, I got a small mortgage to pay everything back.

"Earthen plasters have been pure fun for me and have afforded me a myriad of artistic opportunities. I have sculpted niches; a truth window; an archway over my French doors with Long Island seashells; a headboard over my bed using clay I gathered in New Mexico; and, on my living room wall, a large wave made from Kauai beach glass and shells. On my outer walls, I have also shaped a gecko and some prickly pear cactus from cob and colored them with pottery clay. There are bits of me and my life all over the walls, making the house an even more enjoyable place to live.

"Part of what I desired from this house was community involvement in the spirit of the old barn raisings. It was a real pleasure to meet so many people who were willing to assist in both the wall-raising party and the earthen-plaster party, asking nothing in return but the experience. People came from all over to help. I enjoy knowing that the vast majority of the labor on this house was supplied by people who helped because they cared either about the house or the earth. The earthen plaster party was the best display of cooperation I've ever seen. Now, I'm one of those people who love to participate in wall raisings whenever I can find them."

—Carolyn Roberts
www.ahouseofstraw.com

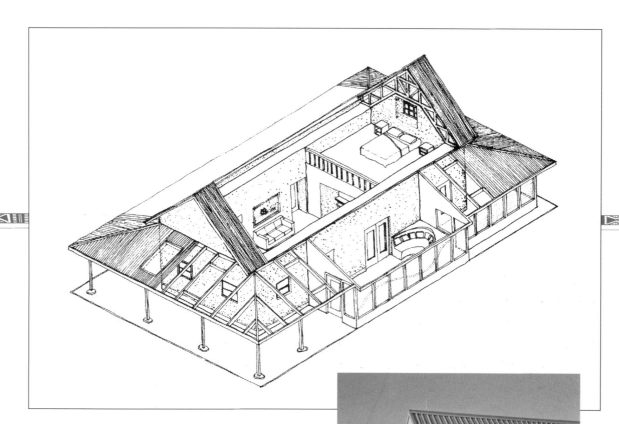

Top: The drawing is a slightly larger version of Carolyn's house with an interior of 900 square feet (83.64 square meters). This is the original plan that inspired her house.

Right: Entry porch.

155

EXPANSION POSSIBILITIES

The plan to the right shows a room with two sleeping/study/wardrobe spaces for young children built under the wraparound roof. This additional space can be constructed without altering the main roof structure. A further extension allows another bathroom/study/bedroom space to be added to the open living/kitchen/dining space. This requires a new gable roof over the expansion. The resulting L-shaped plan generates a possibility for a courtyard enclosure using garden walls and private outdoor living space.

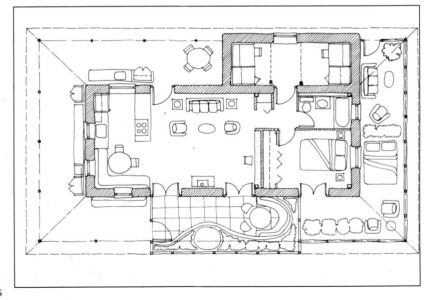

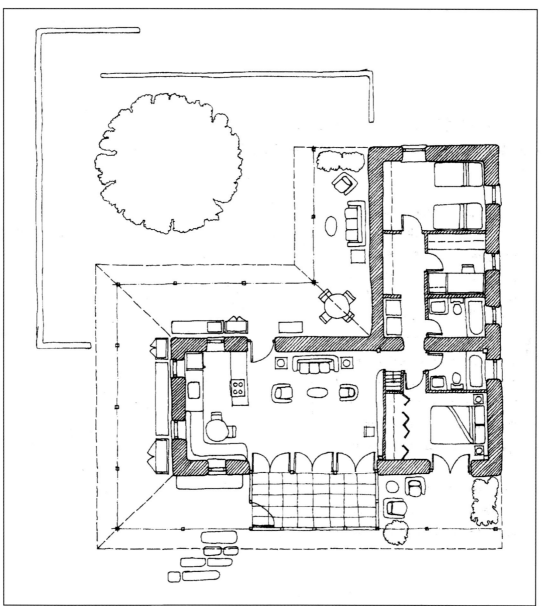

The cabin is 32 x 28 feet (9.75 x 8.53 meters), for a 750-square-foot (69.70-square-meter) interior.

TOM'S CABIN

Crestone, Colorado

"I bought land in Crestone sight unseen and camped out for a week. Traveling a lot as a nurse, I was looking for a home base in a safe community and Crestone fit my requirements.

"Being from the East, I was struck by how brutal the elements could be—harsh wind, blazing heat, mountain cold, and flash storms. My first set of plans was for a two-story cape until, on a blazing day in July, I entered a strawbale house and felt like I had entered an air-conditioned room. Strawbale now provides me with a physical and psychological cocoon. I grew up in a drafty mansion and have been waiting for a snug place for years.

"My little house is 896 square feet (83.27 square meters), was designed by Touson Saryon of Integral Design Studio, and built by Paul Koppana of SkyHawk Construction (John McKean was the site foreman) on a tight budget. Despite the small size, it has a spacious feel with high ceilings and a shoji window that opens to the bedroom. It takes advantage of passive solar, has radiant floor heat, and earthen plaster inside and out. The cabinets are reclaimed Douglas fir, with a Feng Shui design by Robin Cheri of Aspen."

—Tom Deegan

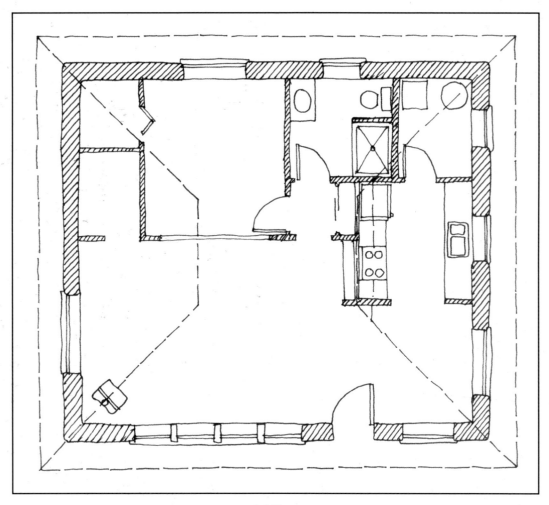

THE PANTRY

A generous pantry can be a useful addition to any small house. It can be the main support hub of the kitchen in that it contains all the necessary components and ingredients that are needed for many a great meal.

One of the marvelous things about pantries is that everything is clearly visible and easy to find. Things are much less likely to disappear into a dark recess or cupboard corner. And in addition to improved visibility and usefulness, a pantry can be significantly less expensive to build than cabinets while providing much more storage space.

Bulk dry goods—rice, beans, pastas, spices and the like—can be easily seen and stored in gallon-sized jars. Beyond food items, pantries can house things used daily but not wanted in the main part of the kitchen, such as recycling bins, brooms and mops, pet foods, and what have you. Even the noisy, bulky refrigerator can be hidden out of sight. With the ample space, one can keep enough extra ingredients to be always prepared for the unexpected mealtime drop-in guest who might otherwise go hungry or be subjected to a marginal plate of food. In short, the pantry can potentially be one of the most essential rooms in the house.

The kitchen pantry. Canelo, Arizona.

LEANNE'S HOME

Moab, Utah

"Sanctuary, refuge, retreat—these are the words that come to mind when I think of my strawbale home. My motivation for all things in life is strongly rooted in a need for simplicity, and this is reflected in the design and furnishings of my home. Designing it required me to intimately connect with my needs and desires, and then allowed me to express them in a very tangible and aesthetic way. There is nothing elaborate, luxurious, or even particularly creative about my home, and yet it conveys a sense of elegant simplicity that satisfies me deeply. I've resisted hanging artwork, choosing instead to enjoy the inherent beauty of the hand-plastered walls—the sensuous curves, the imperfections, and the subtle play of light and texture over their surfaces.

"Perhaps more than any other feature, it is the 6-inch-thick, poured adobe floor that provides the house with the sense of functional beauty that I like to think defines its overall aesthetic. We used clay soil from the site, with no added pigments or clay to color it. It retains its rich chocolate color flecked with bits of gold from chopped straw. I chose to insulate the floor with pumice rather than synthetic materials in order to avoid any unnatural barriers between the earth's energy and my own. This natural mass, along with the plastered bale walls, gives the house a tangible sense of peace, harmony, and healing energy that nearly everyone comments on when they visit for the first time.

"Like all strawbale homes, mine has a story. It was born of a shared love of strawbale building between my ex-husband, Dave Clark,

The vented, hipped roof allows for even wall height on all sides. The exterior plaster is lime.

Opposite: Leanne in her kitchen. The walls are painted with a light colored clay over earth plasters. The floor is a local clay sealed with linseed oil.

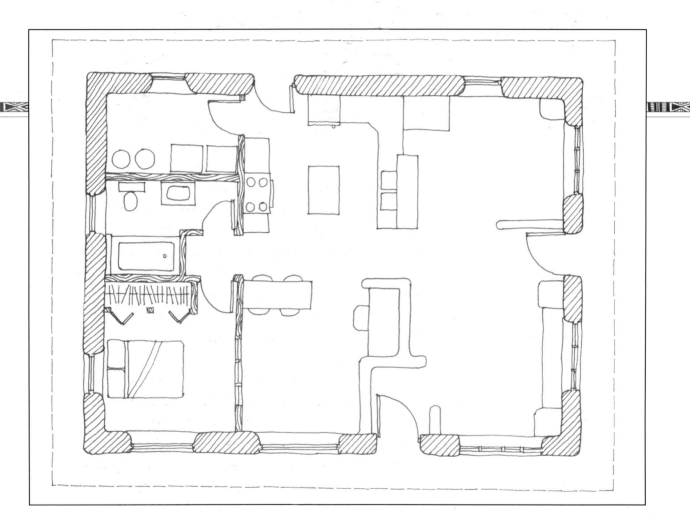

The house is 30 x 25 feet (9.14 x 7.62 meters), for a 600-square-foot (55.76-square-meter) interior.

and me and was the product of a divorce settlement. Dave had built a strawbale home for us during our ten-year marriage, a home we shared for three years. Upon separating, we agreed that he would keep the house in exchange for helping me build a small, simple strawbale home of my own, just one mile away from his. Dave's expertise, craftsmanship, and attention to detail are strongly reflected in the quality and beauty of the house.

"The unusual divorce arrangement proceedings is perhaps the most remarkable aspect of the project. Having already been through the building process together, we were prepared for the typical challenges, frustrations, and problems inherent in such an undertaking. In addition to these difficulties, however, we were faced with maintaining a healthy friendship and working relationship while simultaneously dissolving our marriage. There were times each of us questioned the validity of our arrangement, but it is telling that now, several years after completing the house, we are better friends than ever and continue to support each other in many ways. In fact, it is likely that the project helped each of us uncover and strengthen qualities within ourselves we might not otherwise have come to discover.

"In short, it is the simplicity of my home that makes it beautiful, and the story behind its creation is a testament to the power of cooperation, mutual respect, and shared values. More than a shelter, my home gives me a place to ground, center, heal, and grow. It is my spiritual home as well as my physical home."

—Leanne Trusdale

WAYNE & COLLEEN'S HOUSE

Teton Valley, Idaho

Colleen Smith and
Wayne J. Bingham.

*Opposite: The wrap-
around porch protects
the exterior clay
plasters.*

"Our interest in strawbale construction grew out of our concern for energy efficiency. Our research into energy-efficient building grew into an awareness of sustainable building practices. An urge to build an energy-efficient home of materials that are sustainable increased as we explored these issues.

"As we examined the site conditions, we found that prevalent winds came from the southwest, passive solar orientation was due south, and views were predominantly southeast to the Teton Range. The Hollingshead homestead to the west anchored the place visually, and the rolling grass and grain fields to the north and east held their own hypnotic beauty. How would we place a building here and what would it look and feel like?

"We walked the site many times over several years, exploring for the right place to build and the right kind of structure to respond to the soil, views, and weather. When the irrefutable drive to build overwhelmed us, we went to the land and stayed for three days, walking, feeling, talking, and looking for the right place. We examined alternative ways of achieving solar gain while maintaining prominent views and avoiding challenging weather patterns.

"The summer sun in our high mountain desert can be intense, and the evenings cool down fast when the sun goes down. So a porch wrapped around strawbale walls made sense to us. It would protect us from the sun, provide outdoor living space, and allow the strawbales and the internal thermal mass to moderate and maintain a relatively even temperature inside the house. The porch would also serve to protect the earthen-plastered bales from the weather.

"We wanted the house to sit lightly on the land and allow the rolling surface of the earth to

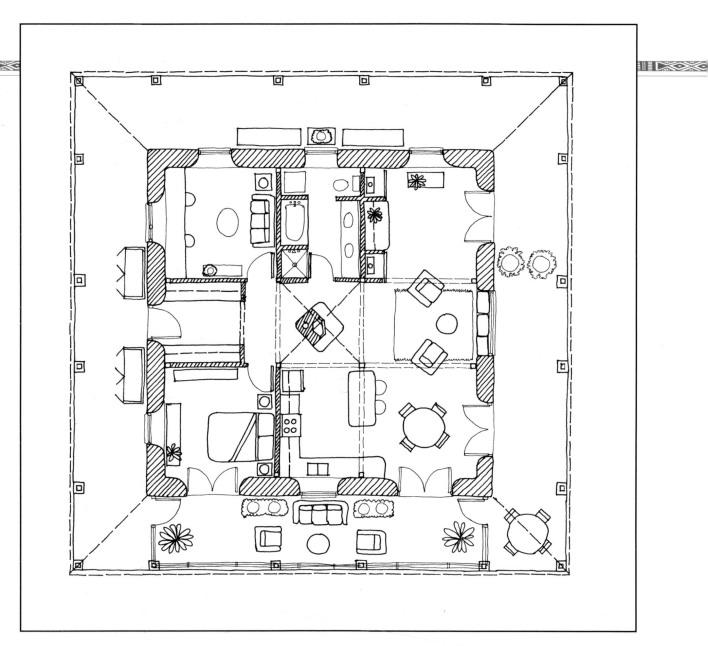

The sides are 34 x 34 feet (10.36 x 10.36 meters) long. The interior square footage is 961 square feet (89.31 square meters).

168

flow unimpeded past the house. We raised the porch surface only 6 inches above the adjacent ground around the entire perimeter to require only one step to grade.

"While working with Athena and Bill Steen on this book, we experienced several houses that deeply impressed us. They were approximately square, had hip roofs, and had wraparound porches. The deep porches were occupied with plants, chairs, tables, firewood, clotheslines, and other apparatus for living outdoors under cover.

"After consideration of many schemes, we settled on one that is 34 feet square (10.36 meters square), which provides 1,156 gross square feet (107.40 gross square meters) and 961 net usable square feet (89.28 square meters). Seventeen percent of the total area is in strawbales and the house is 83 percent efficient. It has a kitchen/living area, one bath, a master bedroom, and study/guestroom. There is a loft for the grandchildren.

"Colleen had researched the area for organic strawbales that were 14 x 18 inches (355 x 457 millimeters). We found a farmer in Blackfoot, about ninety miles away who had grown straw without herbicides or pesticides. Because the crop had matured and there was rain forecast, he decided

to cut the wheat and bail the straw. We had been working to have the house dried-in before taking delivery of the bales. We were able to place the bales under the newly finished roof before the rains. Bale installation took only one week—notching and fitting under the roof and between columns, windows, and doors.

"Several friends called out of the blue and said that they had heard that plastering was about to happen and asked if they could help. Yes! Stan, John, Joe, Susan, and I spent the weekend hand-applying the beautiful chocolate-colored earthen plaster mixed with long fibers of straw. We were at the end of summer, and we wanted it to dry before it could freeze, which would render earthen plasters no good. We were able to apply a rough coat on three walls over a three-day weekend. Brian and I finished the final wall in two days. The first weather coat had taken about one week. The building season had ended and we left for the winter.

"When we returned in June of 2003, we turned our attention to the final plastering on the main house. Sift clay, chop straw, mix clay to water, add straw and sand, and apply to the rough coat applied last year. We had a lot of work to do. We also needed to check proportions,

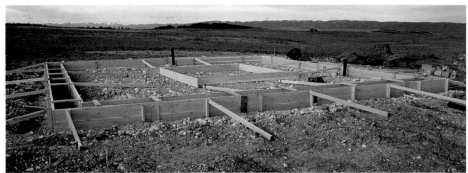

Top: Foundation form work. Dimensions are 34 x 34 feet (10.36 x 10.36 meters), for 961 square feet (89.31 square meters).

Middle, top: The concrete block columns are 13 feet (3.96 meters) apart.

Middle, bottom: The porch structure and roof beams.

Bottom: The structure with bale infill is complete. The cupola helps vent hot air and lets light into the center of the building.

170

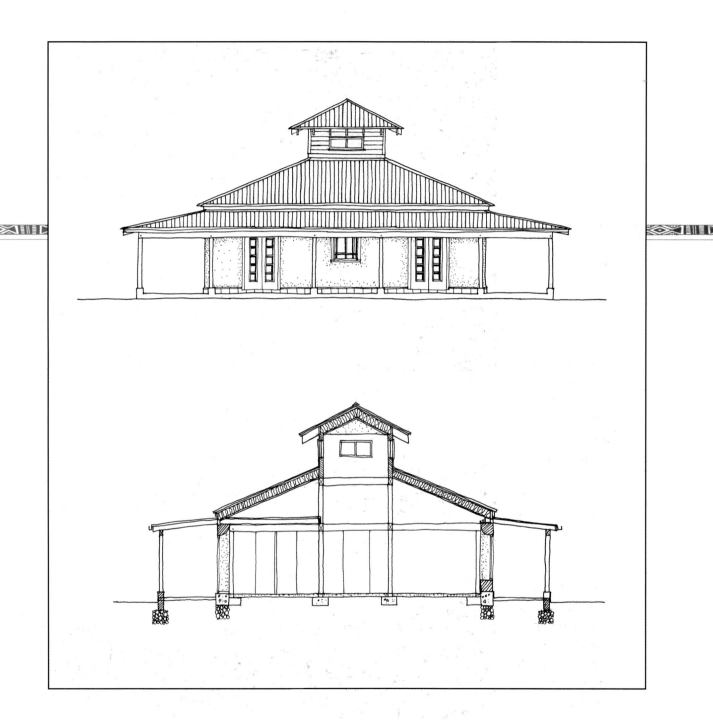

call and ask the Steens about using floats or steel trowels, read about natural plasters, do tests, and define how we wanted to do the work. Out of the research, study, and questioning came a process we are very pleased with. We applied an infill coat of stiff plaster with wood floats to the existing hand-applied rough coat. We then brought the surface to within 1/4 inch (6.35 millimeters) of the finish surface using a plaster that has more sand and less straw, which was sent through the chopper a second time.

"The final coat was applied with a steel trowel with curved corners, and polished with stainless steel Japanese trowels. It is beautiful with soft rounded corners and a bottom edge that flared out to meet the metal drip edge.

"After reading recipes for clay 'alis' paint, we decided to call the Steens again for their advice. Their advice was to start with one part wheat-paste glue, add two parts water, and add clay until it covered our fingers without showing a print. We added one small scoop of burnt umber and about four cups of medium-sized mica flakes. We painted it on with four-inch brushes, allowed it to almost dry, and then polished it with a damp (not wet) sponge.

"Wow! What a difference it made. The alis unified the whole surface, and no joints were visible. Before this, the joints between one day's plastering work and another had been visible, even though we tried diligently to feather them out. The house has a soft sheen from the mica. It invites touch, as everyone who comes to the house demonstrates. Some have said it looks like leather. We think it looks like the earth around the house, but is refined by plastering and polishing. It looks like it belongs to its surroundings.

"Building our house started out as a dream, a desire to do something sustainable, and to build with our hands. Our project then became something physical as we worked with the foundations, concrete, rebar, strawbales, earthen plaster, roofs, wiring, etc.

"Our home has provided meaning for us beyond our wildest expectations. There has been a profound change in our lives' direction and satisfaction since we explored ways of becoming involved in sustainable building and focused on strawbale as a preferred method. Thirty-five years of life energy are focused on building our home. Feeling through our needs, responding to the site, and building the house day by day have been the most satisfying and meaningful experiences of our lives."

—Wayne J. Bingham and Colleen Smith
www.wjbingham.com

BASIC DESIGN GUIDELINES FOR SMALL HOUSES

Designing a house requires time to explore possibilities. Designing a house that is both small and efficient as well as comfortable and beautiful is a challenge, but one that can be well worth the effort. The following are important considerations:

• Design spaces around what one does in the course of a day. Match the size to both the space and the time needed for that activity. Consider additions or downsizes that could be made in the future as family size or needs change. This will result in a dwelling that is much better suited to the occupants than something based on preconceived notions and concepts of what a house or space ought to be.

• Relate rooms or spaces to one another so that the transitions between them are smooth and easy. Not doing so can jeopardize the function of that space and/or create wasted space, like hallways. Remember that transitions can be one of the most creative spaces to play with. It is where two things meet and come together that creates fertile ground for something new and exciting.

• Open floor plans with multifunctional spaces, such as a living/kitchen/dining area or laundry/mudroom/storage room, make a lot of sense. Don't close off spaces unless absolutely necessary. Keep bedrooms small and sized for sleeping, not living. Use alcoves or other design features, like varying floor and ceiling heights, to define a space before creating a separate room.

• Keep the plan and structure simple. Avoid making it unnecessarily complex or curvy. Doing so will help avoid unnecessary costs and material consumption. Use curved features on the interior walls, carefully placed details, and built-in furniture to add interest and character to a rectangular floor plan.

- Rather than spreading out horizontally, utilize the space contained within the roof volume for lofts or mezzanines for living or storage.

- Put a premium on outdoor space whether separate from the house or under a porch. Access to and visual connections between those spaces are vital. They help open up the interior of the building and extend the living area to the outdoors and, most importantly, facilitate the connection with what is truly important.

- Take advantage of the smaller size to incorporate better detailing as well as local, natural, and green materials. Be sensible when it comes to how much money will be spent on the house. Don't attempt to justify an excessively large house just because it was built with good materials and is energy/resource efficient.

- Design for energy efficiency: provide ample insulation, take advantage of solar gain, provide for good ventilation, and make the building airtight. Minimize the surface area of the building, not just the square footage. Allow for lots of light, both daylight and well-thought-out artificial light.

HOW SMALL CAN A HABITABLE DWELLING BE?

It is worth noting the minimum requirements for habitable space noted in the International Residential Code. They are an attempt to provide the most basic but sensible guidelines for making a dwelling habitable. Far from randomly chosen, these dimensions have very pragmatic reasons behind them.

- A dwelling needs to have at least one room with a floor area not less than 120 square feet (11.15 square meters). A living area in this case might be thought to contain a place for sitting and eating, assuming that there is an additional bedroom. The space required for a small table and two chairs and an additional sitting area essentially consume that space.

- Any additional habitable rooms except kitchens shall have an area of not less than 70 square feet (6.51 square meters). They shall not be less than 7 feet (2.13 meters) in any dimension. In the case of a bedroom, the length of space needed for the length of a bed will be approximately 7 feet (2.13 meters). Any less than that obviously won't work. An additional 3 feet (.91 meters) will be needed for the width of a single bed, so that leaves 4 feet (1.22 meters) for entry, nightstand, closet, and the like.

- A kitchen must be more than 50 square feet (4.65 square meters). A kitchen usually has a stove, sink, and refrigerator. Even if these were clustered all along one wall, and assuming that there was just 2 feet (610 millimeters) of counter space between each of the above, you'd have consumed at least 23 square feet (2.14 square meters) before allowing any space to stand. When you allow enough floor space in front of the

Interior of Bill and Athena Steen's guesthouse—the Canelo Project Bed and Breakfast.

counter and appliances to simply open the doors without banging the door up against a facing wall, the balance of the 50 square feet (4.65 square meters) is already used up.

• A water-closet compartment must be at least 30 inches (762 millimeters) wide and have a space at least 24 inches (610 millimeters) to the front of the water closet. It must be wide enough to allow placement of the toilet and enough space to the front for clearance of one's knees. There's nothing worse than banging them into the door when sitting.

• Ceilings in habitable spaces need to be at least 7 feet (2.13 meters) high. In rooms with sloping ceilings, the prescribed ceiling height is required in only half the area but cannot be less than 5 feet (1.52 meters). Anything below that can be used for other purposes but cannot be considered part of the habitable space. Standard door height is 80 inches (2,032 millimeters), add to that a 2 x 4-inch (51 x 102-millimeter) lintel and you have a 7-foot (2.13-meter) ceiling.

CLUSTERED COMPOUNDS

Clay shelves worked into the edge of a window opening. Palominas, Arizona.

Where place and climate allow, several small buildings can sometimes make more sense than one large one. Constructing smaller structures, one at a time, can be less intimidating and more manageable, and therefore less stressful—physically, mentally, emotionally, and financially. In addition, separate structures allow the opportunity for clustering buildings or developing a compound, which can be more inviting and intimate than large monolithic structures.

Building in stages allows for gradual expenditure, making it easier to avoid a mortgage. When the first phase has been paid for and more money is available, one can move on to the next phase. Cost and budget miscalculations can be learned from and corrected before attempting something else. Building in stages also allows one to rest and recuperate between each stage.

As with any undertaking, there is a learning curve. When building separate structures, improvements and lessons learned from one can be applied to the next. Experimentation with different techniques and methods is also much more likely to happen on smaller buildings. Another common phenomenon is when owner-builders to discover that a smaller space is more than adequate for their needs and consequently don't build anything larger. It's often difficult for people to translate the size of what has been drawn on paper into actual physical space, so designs end up much larger than what is really needed. Sometimes people who are initially apprehensive about being in too small a space may be less so once they are actually living in it.

A series of buildings creates great opportunity to develop outdoor living spaces, such as courtyards and seasonal patios. Garden walls, screens, plantings, and overhead shaded or covered roofs can all further enclose, extend, or define the usable area.

John Hammond's compound with bale wall. California.

FRED & BETSY'S HOME

Patagonia, Arizona

"We chose strawbale because of its inherent sustainability factor, and also for the challenge of using a new building material. The organic feel of strawbale was another appeal. And at the risk of sounding self-righteous, it also seemed like an environmentally friendly thing to do, one we could share with others to serve as inspiration and example.

"After spending several winters in Mexico, avoiding those frigid Montana winters, we landed in Patagonia, Arizona. We decided to try wintering there and build a small strawbale house. After attending a strawbale workshop in Butte, Montana, and then one with the Steens, we were convinced and empowered enough to try building a house of straw! The configuration of two small buildings side-by-side appealed to us. This plan allows us to spend lots of time outside on the broad porches and have space separate from each other (which is something to consider when thinking about retirement). This 'compound' plan used strawbale walls around the whole place.

"We built the first building (the casita), with a 544-square-foot (50.56-square-meter) interior, in 1998. We lived in it for two winters before we committed to selling our home in Montana and moving to Arizona *en todo* (totally). Then we built the big house, 946 square feet (87.92 square meters), inside in 2001. So the casita is now our guest house/studio/TV space/yoga room. We decided on small buildings because that's what strawbale best lends itself to.

"Before our strawbale experience, we had lived in solar houses and over-insulated homes. Living in strawbale is by far the best experience to date. Its organic, lumpy look and feel is so

Top, left: Entry walkway into the compound.

Top, middle: Garage painted with lime-casein paints. The garden ball is ceramic.

Top, right: The Magee compound comprised of the guest house/ studio, main house, and a garden wall. The strawbale wall is capped with Mexican tiles. The lime plaster was frescoed with red iron oxide and then stained with ferrous sulfate.

pleasing. The swing in temperature is the smallest we have ever experienced. Granted we live in a quiet area, but the superinsulated strawbale keeps us in a silent, serene space that we don't take for granted.

"Thinking about what we'd do differently, it would be better to use more glazing in the main living area of the large house, if that would be possible without compromising the strength of the bales. The master bedroom in the bigger house could be a bit larger, but having written that I feel like I'm whining. None of that!

"We used as much natural material in the houses as possible, all lime and mud plasters with the addition of nopal (prickly pear cactus) gel in these. Floors are tile, with lots of tile in the bathrooms. Hey, we're near Mexico! We used all

natural paints (casein and wheat paste). Bill Steen always said that our project was a showcase for Home Depot products, yet with an artistic flair and outcome. It's not so much that many of our materials came from Home Depot as much as they are materials that were easily accessible. We didn't go to any great lengths to use exotic or custom items.

"The casita cost $35,000, while the larger house cost about $65,000. The $65,000 includes a strawbale wall around the compound and a more expensive kitchen than we have in the casita. We built the houses ourselves with the help of Erasmo and his nephew Carlos from Patagonia, Arizona, who know how to do everything. When we first started building, there was no electricity or water on-site, so we used

180

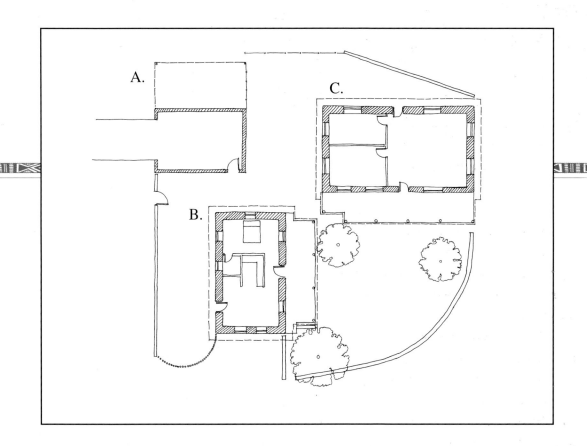

A. The garage/storage is cement block.

B. The smaller casita is 21 x 36 feet (6.40 x 10.97 meters), with a 544-square-foot (50.56-square-meter) interior. The cost was around $35,000.

C. The big house is 26 x 47 feet (7.92 x 14.33 meters), with a 946-square-foot (87.92-square-meter) interior. It cost about $65,000.

battery-powered tools and water from a nearby stock tank. How many carpenters do you know who would go along with that plan?

"Each structure took about five months to complete. Hey, if a couple of retired over-sixty-year-olds can do this, so can you. The building industry needs to be demystified. Strawbale can do that. Take back the ability to design and construct your own dwelling."

—Betsy Magee

Top, left: Dining room with red iron-oxide casein paint.

Top, right: Guest-house with porch.

Bottom, left: The bale courtyard wall with lime plaster colored with ferrous sulfate and iron oxide.

Bottom, right: Bed is built from bales. The walls are painted with a yellow oxide casein paint.

182

PORCHES

Porches can economically add useful space to a building, protect the walls from rain and excessive sun, facilitate the use of earthen plasters, and help transform an ordinary box of a building into something much more useful and appealing. Some of their many uses include eating and sleeping areas, outdoor kitchens, utility areas like mudrooms and laundry, storage, and potting tables.

The tempered glass from salvaged insulated patio door units (free or next to free) or another type of clear glazing could be used over the windows in place of the opaque roofing so as not to restrict light from reaching the windows. Depending on the climate, these may or may not be shaded during the warmer months of the year.

Of course the glass could be used for all the porch roofing and would also be good for rainwater harvesting. However, a porch that is roofed entirely with glass might be a hellish inferno. The windows could be shaded with mats or shade cloth, or painted with whitewash in summer. Deciduous vines could also be enticed to grow over the glazed areas.

For heating, the porch on the equator-facing wall can be enclosed with glass to make it into an attached greenhouse/solar furnace. Or in areas where wind-driven, almost-horizontal rain or snow is common, the walls of the porch could be enclosed with operable windows/doors, such as those wonderful, salvaged, divided-lite single-glazed wooden window sashes that don't really belong on a superinsulated building. Roll-up rain screens for the sides of open porches would also be an option in places where the climate is not so severe.

Well-lived-in porch on old adobe house. Patagonia, Arizona.

PAUL'S COMPOUND

~~~~~~

Crestone, Colorado

Opposite: Interior photos of the house.

"Working with straw, plaster, and adobe is a real joy. I've been a building contractor since 1987 and have been working with bales since 1996, but this was the first time I got to build a home for myself. Strawbale was a natural progression from the well-insulated, passive solar structures I was building. The soft, fluid, undulations in strawbale walls mimic nature, feel organic, and are environmentally renewable because you are using a waste material. Now I specialize in bale building.

"I was first introduced to strawbale building when I was involved with an organic farm community in North Carolina. They wanted to build with bales, so I sought out bale experience. That is what brought me to Crestone, which is a mecca for bale building.

"Crestone lies at 8,000 feet above sea level in the San Luis Valley in south-central Colorado at the base of the Sangre de Christo Mountains. We have 320 sunny days a year, so passive and active solar are always important considerations for any home we build. Passive solar is great, but you need to retain the heat. My past experience building superinsulated homes has been an asset in helping me to learn to skillfully handle the thermal efficiency of the building envelope.

"My home and collection of outbuildings is an experiment—and a continual process. Everything we do for clients we've tried before, often at my place first. Having no building codes in Crestone has allowed us to try new things without having to conform to stringent standards.

"With a healthy respect for experimentation,

185

I began building my own residence: four buildings, including a home, studio, shed, and sauna. Building a compound can be economical because you can pay as you go. You can tackle (and make mistakes on) small freestanding structures rather than one monster project that can become daunting. Small structures encourage experimentation. For example, my studio was the first time I used load-bearing bales on edge. Now I employ that method all the time. Plus, some spaces, such as shops, garages, and art spaces, simply don't lend themselves to being attached to a home because of fumes, noise, etc. I also love interacting with the outdoors between buildings, like seeing the stars overhead when I walk from the sauna to my house at night.

"After many months of planning, building my own home was a joyful experience—even though we started in mid-March 2001, planning to be finished by July, but didn't finish until October. The main house is a 1,200-square-foot (111.48-square-meter) passive solar building with a radiant floor. Utilities average twenty-five dollars a month and a half cord of wood in the winter. The first floor is an infill structure with bales on edge; the second story uses the bales in a load-bearing capacity. A lot of local wood was used in the frame and interior trim. The hip roof has raised heel trusses and R-60 cellulose insulation. The house has earthen plasters, adobe floors, and an

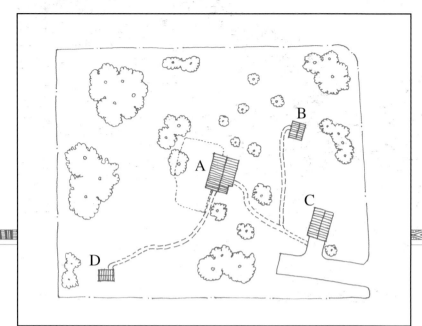

Site plan for the compound:
A. Main house
B. Wood shop
C. Storage
D. Sauna

adobe wall between the kitchen and greenhouse.

"I grew up with saunas, so building one on my property was a priority. In the Finnish tradition, the sauna is a sacred space where family and friends come together, cleanse, purify, and relax. The sauna we built has created a community of people who regularly come together to share these values. It is a treasure in a remote small town. Often it also serves as an informal information hub on alternative building. I've built several saunas but this was the first strawbale one. I consulted Bert Olaui Jalasjaa's book *The Art of Sauna Building*. The design is mine. It has a sand floor with redwood slated decking. It has load-bearing bales on edge with earthen plaster inside and out. We used aspen 1 x 4 inch (25 x 102 millimeter) for the benches because it is cooler to sit on than other woods. The interior of the sauna uses 1 x 6-inch (25.40 x 152.40-millimeter) tongue and groove cedar.

"I learn from every project. Here are some of the lessons learned from building my home:

• When in doubt, bring the floor elevation a little higher to protect bales and earthen floors.
• I used concrete stucco on my stick-framed south wall, but earthen plasters would have worked just fine.

187

The strawbale sauna, with a 12 x 13-foot (3.66 x 3.96-meter) exterior, and vaulted roof. Interior square footage is 156 square feet (14.51 square meters).

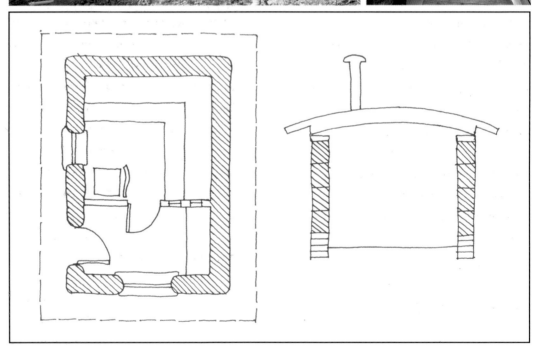

• The blueprints show my wood stove next to the stairway, but we moved it to the southwest corner of the living room. This was a major Feng Shui fix that has worked so well I couldn't imagine it in its initial place.

• Always test with samples first when trying something different. At the last minute, we changed our oiling procedure for my adobe floor. Instead of using three to four coats of linseed, we used BioShield Penetrating Oil #5. This oil did not penetrate the way the linseed oil does; hence my floors are a little weak.

• Pre-wire for computer network lines and DSL.

• If you want to use your radiant floor heat, but do not want to pay for the propane, add more solar panels. I'll be adding three more this summer just for floor heat.

• Skylights over a vertical glass walled greenhouse don't make up for sloped-glass south walls. Mine were a waste of time and money.

"Many wonderful people helped me on these buildings. Some of them include architect Touson Saryon of Integral Design Studio; Talmath Mesenbrink of MudCrafters Construction; and Randy Seismore of Entropy Limited. I would also like to thank Ben Ummer and Don Lewis for foundation and bale work; Jonathon Bruce and Anikke Storm for earthen plasters and floors; Mark Schneider for the redwood floor and firebrick; and Robin Cheri for her Feng Shui–design advice."

—Paul Koppana
SkyHawk Construction
Crestone, Colorado

Top, left: The wood shop has a 25 x 18-foot (7.62 x 5.49-meter) exterior. Interior is 330 square feet (30.67 square meters).

Top, middle: Storage shed, 15 x 10-foot (4.57 x 3.05-meter) exterior, with arched roof similar to the sauna. Interior is 84 square feet (7.81 square meters).

Top, right: Interior of wood shop.

TOM & SATOMI'S LANDERLAND

Satomi and Tom Lander.

"For seven years, Satomi and I had rented a room and shared the kitchen in a three-story mountain lodge.

"After a couple of years, we bought the lot next door, which we call LanderLand. We had been working slowly on the master plan when we began the extensive infrastructure, installing all the buried utilities. During this time, we also built a small load-bearing strawbale pump house, a recycled garage door panel shop, and started on what we call the Big House, a 640-square-foot (59.48-square-meter) hybrid timber frame with an exterior bale wrap. The roof was finished at the end of 2002, a major step, but we still have two years to go to finish.

"Satomi had had enough. 'We need to move next door,' she said. 'Why did you build the timber frame instead of building a house where we could live?'

"We had built two other structures on the property, one was an 8 x 17–foot-interior (2.44 x 5.18–meter-interior) material rack, and the other a 10 x 13–foot-interior (3.05 x 3.96–meter-interior) load-bearing strawbale storage building that was in process. 'So why don't we live in the storage building?' she asked. We did a study of where the furniture would go. I could build an outdoor shower and a composting toilet. Maybe we could buy a tent for the kitchen. 'What about winter?' asked Satomi. 'When will this all be done? Tom, I want to be in by summer.'

"As work on the former storage shed, soon to be bedroom, progressed, we realized we needed more space. I kept eyeing the material rack. I really had to convince Satomi to let me start yet another building. She agreed but only if we could move in by June.

"It would be tight. We needed space for

Timber frame of future house.

the queen-sized bed. There went half the floor space. A toilet, shower, and kitchen would fill up the other half. Put the water heater and electric panel outside and it would be doable. While I built, Satomi plastered both buildings. On June 1, 2003, we moved in. With the linseed oil still drying on the earthen floor, Satomi cooked our first meal, and we spent our first night in our very own little strawbale house. Our time had come, so what took so long?

"We are so happy living next door on our own property. Why didn't we build a small house to live in years ago and then start the timber frame? Good question. We spend so much time outdoors that we really don't need a big place anyway. We sleep, shower, and eat. A bigger kitchen would be nice but this way there is only room for one in the kitchen so I don't have to cook. We use the deep windowsill as a shelf for the bread machine, toaster, and coffee grinder with enough space to store our fruit. The pump house has been converted from tool storage to our food and beer pantry.

"Our little strawbale is so cozy and with the radiant heat we use less then a gallon of propane a month. Small does not limit quality. Our little buildings are elegant with lots of craftsmanship details, and the earthen plasters and woodwork inspire the many who visit."

—Tom & Satomi Lander
www.landerland.com

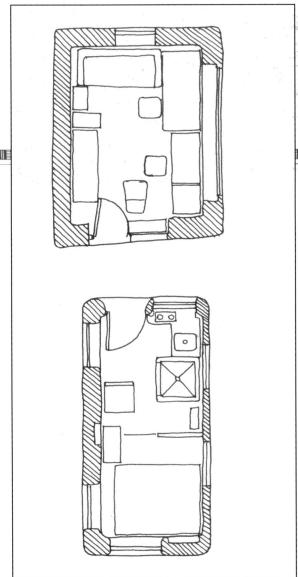

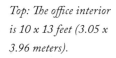

Top: The office interior is 10 x 13 feet (3.05 x 3.96 meters).

Bottom: The living area is 136 square feet (12.64 square meters).

193

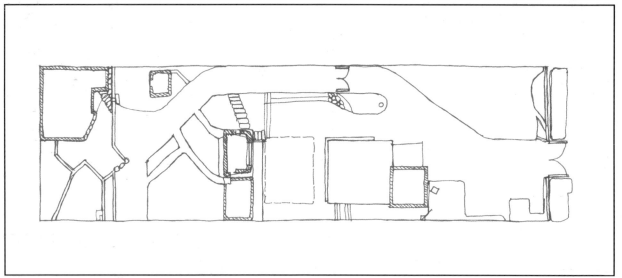

OUTDOOR ROOMS

Clustering buildings provides the opportunity to develop a variety of interesting and useful spaces between and around them, such as courtyards and other outdoor "rooms" that can be used for cooking, eating, conversing, working, relaxing, sleeping, and sitting. Using the walls of the buildings, these areas could be arranged and enclosed to suit the activity and the time of day or year. Porches or trellised coverings could act as transition spaces from indoors to outdoors as well as passageways to link the buildings to each other and to outdoor areas.

Outdoor pavilion and courtyard, with a sunroom on the southeast.

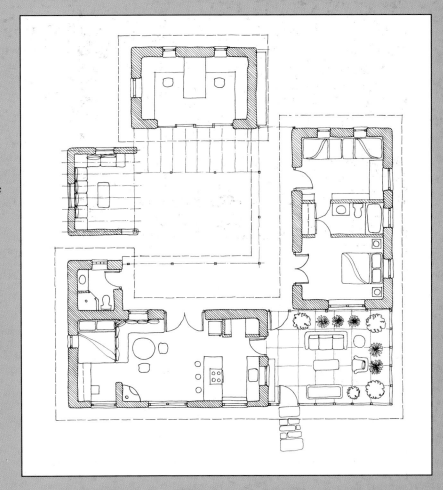

JOHN & SUSAN'S COMPOUND

Ganmain, Australia

"Like most strawbale builders around the world today, our journey began with an article on strawbale building in a local magazine that referenced *The Straw Bale House* by the Steens, Bainbridge, and Eisenberg. This led us to a whole new way of life and a complete change from building homes for the wealthy to running strawbale workshops for those Aussies who want to have a go at building their own homes. This journey continues to this day, and we have made many wonderful and genuine friendships with people all around Australia.

"Our own personal financial situation also led us to Ganmain where land is cheap and there is plenty of straw. Our aim was to start a happy new life as a middle-aged couple, mortgage free. The journey has also led us to the United States

for research. Once we discovered Christopher Alexander's book *A Pattern Language,* we knew what we wanted and used several of the patterns to design and build our own strawbale home in Ganmain.

"We needed some land where we could build our own home and at the same time teach others how to build theirs. We decided to build several small pavilions using the low-cost load-bearing strawbale walls, joining them together with covered and sometimes enclosed walkways. Pavilion-style building suits most of the climate conditions around Australia since we do not have snow or permafrost. We designed our home to keep cool in the summer, orienting each of our seven pavilions according to the function of each, determining the number of hours we

Opposite: The living area and the marriage room of Jack's Flat.

197

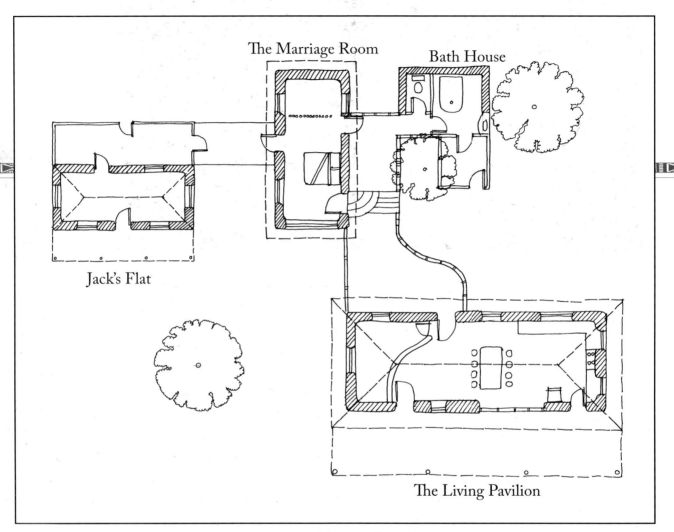

The Marriage Room

Bath House

Jack's Flat

The Living Pavilion

Jack's Flat: 26.25 x 24.8 feet (8.00 x 7.56 meters).
Living pavilion: 25 x 23 feet (7.62 x 7.01 meters).
Marriage room: 29.52 x 17.88 feet (9.00 x 5.45 meters).
Bath house: 26.24 x 24.8 feet (8.00 x 7.56 meters).

Total square footage is 3,278 square feet (304.65 square meters).

would be using a particular pavilion for sleeping and waking.

"Our kitchen, dining, and living room space faces north with enough glass windows to give good passive solar heating off the slate floor during the winter nights. The south wall will have a rain forest pergola, and the north wall will have a deciduous pergola for cool air through the south wall in the summer and heat through the north wall in winter.

"The bathhouse pavilion is connected to the marriage room by an enclosed, covered walkway. Jack's Flat is a self-contained cottage joined to the marriage room by an open walkway and functions as a guesthouse for family and friends who visit. A stand-alone round house functions as my sacred space, a small pavilion for our dog, Jessica, and the seventh pavilion will be Susan's studio for inspirational furniture making.

"What we call Jack's Flat was one of several buildings built around 1838 on a farm called by the same name located near Gundaroo, which is by Canberra. The original photo shows Jack's Flat before we moved to Ganmain. It was a slab house made from ironbark slabs hand split and

Top, left: The living pavilion is heated by the winter sun that pours in through equator-facing (north) windows and is stored for the night in the slate floor. The room contains the kitchen as well as the eating and main living area where most of our waking hours are spent.

Top, right: The marriage room with bamboo ceiling and dressing-area screen.

199

The current Jack's Flat.

adzed by the old timers. The reason it survived was that the timber used was termite resistant.

"In rebuilding Jack's Flat at Ganmain, we reused everything, including the doors; windows; verandahs, back and front; as well as all the roof timbers, which were stringybark. We also used the original corrugated iron, which was the second roofing material used since corrugated iron didn't come to Australia until the 1870s. The original roof was bark. We used wheat straw for the load-bearing walls. The total cost of materials was $1,500 Aussie. The renders used were earth/chaff for the first two coats with a lime putty/sand/oxide mix for the two finish coats.

"Two Christmases ago a car traveling at forty kilometers per hour hit Jack's Flat, but it left only two major cracks. The building still sits on cypress pine piers and joists with the original timber floor."

—John Glasford
www.strawbale.archinet.com.au/

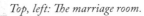

Top, left: The marriage room.

Top, right: The dog house.

Top, middle: Susan's studio is used primarily for inspirational furniture making.

Bottom, middle: John's stand-alone round hut is his sacred space with a TV dedicated for his entertainment where he can watch the "footie" and cricket matches in peace.

Bottom: The bath house functions very well. In the winter, the sun beats down on the earth rendered rear wall and heats the room.

PHOTOGRAPHY CREDITS

Wayne J. Bingham, 10–12, 38–39, 40, 44–45, 76, 79, 124, 148, 152, 155, 165–166, 170

Darrel DeBoer, 19

Bill Ellzey, 158–159, 184, 186, 188, 189 (center)

John Glassford, 196, 199–201

Jim Gritz, 189 (left and right)

Joelee Joyce, 26 (bottom left), 27

Patricia Kearn, 140–141

Joe Kennedy, 28 (bottom center)

Chris Morgan, 84–87

Carolyn Roberts, 149

Dirk Scharmer, 112–114, 115 (top right)

John Swearingen, 80–82, 83 (top)

Kim Thompson, 28 (top, bottom left, and bottom right)

Paul Wiener, 147 (left)

RESOURCES

The Last Straw Journal and Annual Resource Guide
PO Box 22706
Lincoln, NE 68542-2706
ph 402 483 5135
fax 402 483 5161
<thelaststraw@thelaststraw.org>
www.thelaststraw.org

The Annual Resource Guide includes a thorough listing of human, organizational, internet, book, video and product resources related to straw bale construction.

Internet Resources for Discussion:

Strawbale Social Club/SB-r-us
http://groups.yahoo.com/groups/SB-r-us
or send an email to <SB-r-us-subscribe@yahoo.com>
Choose the plain text option to avoid advertisements.

The Strawbale Construction List
<strawbale@listserv.repp.org>
archives at: http://listserv.repp.
org/archives/strawbale.html